Bloom-Again
Orchids

Maudiae Paphiopedilum

Bloom-Again
Orchids

50 Easy-Care Orchids That Flower Again and Again and Again

judywhite

Vanda

Odontocidium

Multiflora Phalaenopsis

TIMBER PRESS
Portland * London

Text by judywhite. Photographs by judywhite/GardenPhotos.com.

Published in 2009 by Timber Press, Inc.

The Haseltine Building
133 S.W. Second Avenue, Suite 450
Portland, Oregon 97204-3527
www.timberpress.com

2 The Quadrant
135 Salusbury Road
London NW6 6RJ
www.timberpress.co.uk

ISBN-13: 978-1-60469-055-2

Printed in China

Library of Congress Cataloging-in-Publication Data
White, Judy.
Bloom-again orchids : 50 easy-care orchids that flower again
and again and again / judywhite.
p. cm.
Includes bibliographical references and index.
ISBN 978-1-60469-055-2
1. Orchids. 2. Orchids—Varieties. I. Title.
SB409.W528 2009
635.9'344--dc22   2009022893

A catalog record for this book is also available from the British Library.

For my sister, Joan White,
and my brother-in-law, David Weisbrod,
the most generous people I know.

My life would be impoverished if your love were not in it.

CONTENTS

Miltonia

Vuylstekeara

Dendrobium

Brassia

Zygopetalum

Neostylis

Sarcochilus

Fragrant *Phalaenopsis*

Phalaenopsis

Paphiopedilum

Aliceara

Multiflora Phalaenopsis

Ascocenda

Cymbidium

Disa

Colmanara

ACKNOWLEDGMENTS

This book would not exist if Tom Fischer and the good folk at Timber Press hadn't come to me with the idea in the first place. My foremost thanks, therefore, to all of them. Special thanks go to Helen Townes, whose gentle editorial hand was greatly appreciated, and to designer Laura Shaw.

Orchid-growing friends from all over the world have contributed knowledge, tips, and time, as well as consoling laughter over the years, when, as is inevitable no matter how experienced you get, an orchid or two is accidentally murdered. These invaluable compatriots are too many to name. Let me just say a general thank you to the North Jersey Orchid Society, who first welcomed me in, as well as to the Deep Cut Orchid Society, and the Greater New York Orchid Society, and hope those unnamed know how much they meant. I do want to thank in particular Marni Turkel, one of the finest growers—and superb potter—I've ever had the pleasure of knowing.

Deep and immense appreciation goes to the American Orchid Society, which every day strives to help thousands of beginner to advanced orchid growers. Special mention must go to the AOS's most excellent Jim Watson, and to my dear friend and former AOS Executive Director, Lee Cooke; both were always first to lend a hand.

I was privileged to photograph with abandon the pretty mugs of the orchids at Longwood Gardens over many years, usually under the good graces of former orchid curator, Mike Owen. I am grateful to Tom Purviance and John Salventi at Parkside Orchid Nursery for opening their greenhouses to me for some last-minute photos; thanks to my old friend Marc Hachadourian of the New York Botanical Garden for aiding that endeavor. I thank also head grower

Robert Palmer of Sun Bulb/Better-Gro, who was generous with his time in discussing current and future orchid marketing trends for this book. The online community of OrchidBoard.com was also a fun and interesting resource.

Nearest to heart, I thank the powers-that-be for my mother, Ermalinda White, my sister, Joan White, bro-in-law David Weisbrod, nephew Jonathan Weisbrod, my sister, Janet White, who left us too early, and my father, the late great Jim White, as well as my married-into family of Doris Rice, Lizzie Rice Stokes, Carl Stokes, and Montague Stokes, who arrived during the making of this book, and beloved friends on both sides of the ocean: Jeanine Babcock, Bill Kopp, Rachel Kopp, Kathi and Bob Rogers, Fiona Gilsenan, Alan and Linda Detrick, Ian and Jude Hodgson, Graeme Bald, Carol and John Parfitt, Carry Akroyd, Gordon Monk, Agris and Gunta Krumins, Joy Larkcom and Don Pollard, and the late great Paddy Kitchen. They not only kept me awash in white light, funny e-mails, good food, and convivial moments, but in their own inimitable ways, usually unbeknownst even to them, these dear and talented people were instrumental in helping me count down from fifty in finishing this book.

And, finally, though certainly first, I thank Graham Rice for his constant commiseration, editorial input, keen insights, countless mugs of tea and unexpected glasses of wine, as well as—most importantly—his wry humor and endless love. He of all people knows exactly how much it takes to write a book.

INTRODUCTION

Once upon a time, you needed a pot of gold to be able to call an orchid your own. Thankfully, those days are long gone. Now you can't even go to the supermarket without tripping over an orchid. They're everywhere, from big box stores to garden centers, florists and orchid nurseries, on eBay and Amazon.

Today, it's not unusual to find orchids sold flowering in pots and baskets, packaged unbloomed in miniscule pots inside net bags (nicknamed "Baggy Babies"), or even trapped tightly in plastic blister packs like socket wrenches. That they survive and thrive shows, despite their exotic and fragile appearance, how tough orchids really are.

Orchids have been transformed from priceless to popular for several reasons beyond just their ruggedness. First, we figured out how to sow and grow their seeds, which need sterile, laboratory conditions. Then, we learned how to clone them—again, in sterile conditions. That made it possible to create literally millions of plants from one original, quickly and relatively cheaply.

And, during all these scientific breakthroughs, we've also been doing things by hand: taking pollen from one orchid plant and putting it on another, making over a hundred thousand kinds of artificial hybrids.

Add those factors together and you begin to understand where all those *Phalaenopsis* Moth Orchids come from.

The explanation goes further. Because orchids have the unique ability to interbreed among different species and even different types, we've been able to create groups of orchids that would never exist in nature. The aim has been plants with lots of easy-to-grow hybrid vigor and spectacular flowers, gorgeous orchids that are incredible survivors.

This mission has been particularly successful with the wide range of *Cattleya*-type orchids, as well as within all the interrelated *Oncidium*, the latter of which are often sold just as "Intergeneric Orchids." You'll find the most dramatic variety within these two types than probably any other. Together with *Phalaenopsis*, these three major groups dominate the orchid plant mass markets.

Some orchids, however, are still partially or totally resistant to being cloned, and you see far fewer of their kind on the box-store scene. These include the easy-to-grow tropical ladyslippers (*Paphiopedilum*), among many others. Be sure to seek them out too, or you'll miss some of the great treasures of the orchid world.

This book has a mission, too—to help you discover some of the more commonly available, easy-to-grow orchids, to aid in identifying plants that have no labels (as is all too often the case), and to assist in deciphering the sometimes incomprehensible names on the labels of plants that actually have them. Oh, yes, and to tell you how to grow and bloom them—and have them bloom again and again.

So go ahead, pick up an orchid or two, or twelve, or all of the fifty easy types I've chosen here. They are definitely addictive. Give them as gifts, and throw in this book. We've got an exciting new world of orchids ahead of us.

Some Orchid Basics

If you're new to orchids, it can be a bit of a jolt getting used to some of the unfamiliar terminology, strange and tongue-twisting names, and the ways orchids are different from other kinds of houseplants. Here's some help.

How Orchids Grow

First of all, most orchids grow in the tropics, attached to the side of a tree for support. The term for this is *epiphyte*.

Time to repot: After flowers fade and new roots appear, repot this sympodial orchid (*Cattleya* type) climbing over the edge of its clay pot.

Some, however, grow in the ground, although in a very loose, well-drained soil. These types are *terrestrial*. Others grow attached to rocks. They're called *lithophytes*. For growing orchids in pots, we generally use chunks of bark as potting mix, often with various additives (moss, perlite, charcoal; packaged mixes vary), for a fast-draining alternative.

Whatever they grow in—or on—in nature, orchids rarely sit in water. Instead, water and random nutrients race by, and orchids grab them, often with thick roots, and store them in special water-saving parts. Many orchids have thickened growths below their leaves for this purpose, called *pseudobulbs*. They also often have fleshy, water-retentive leaves. These are the most camel-like orchids, needing water only about once a week, and a coarse potting mix so that water drains very quickly. Those with finer roots and less obvious ways of storing water need water more often, and a finer potting mix to hold more water. Plastic pots also retain water longer than clay pots.

Orchids grow older in two basic ways. Those with pseudobulbs make new growths alongside the older ones, kind of like walking along. They're called *sympodial*, and classic types are *Cattleya* and *Oncidium*. You can divide a sympodial type between the growths to make separate plants. When you repot a sympodial orchid, you gauge how much room it's going to need over the next year or two to walk forward, and choose a pot accordingly.

The other type grows upward, making new leaves atop one another. It's called *monopodial*, and a classic example is *Phalaenopsis*. You generally can't divide monopodial orchids. When repotting them into fresh mix, often you can use the same sized pot.

Other orchid parts have specific names. Those that look like flower petals are actually a combination of two pet-

A healthy monopodial orchid (*Angraceum*) showing normal aerial roots; it's not necessary (or even possible, sometimes) to make sure all orchid roots are in the pot.

als and three *sepals*. An orchid also has a modified petal called the *lip*, which is the landing platform for pollinators, so it's often big and flamboyant to attract them. These six parts alternate: if you start at the bottom with the lip, the next part is a sepal, then a petal, then sepal, then petal, then sepal, and back to the lip. Some types of orchids (*Disa*, *Paphiopedilum*) fuse various petals and sepals together, making for a completely different look, but most orchids have the six-part configuration. The parts in the center of the flower above the lip are the sexual organs, contained in a unique orchid structure called the *column*.

Light

Orchids fall into three standard categories of how much sunlight they need to bloom. Avoid northern windows; they are too dark for orchids. You can use the other windows, adjusting how close or far away the plants are from the glass and/or using a see-through curtain.

Low: Casts a soft shadow when you put your hand between the window and the plant. Eastern window, or indirect, filtered, or morning light of southern and western windows all can work well.

Medium: Casts a medium to sharp shadow. Unfiltered morning light is usually good.

High: Casts a strong, sharp shadow, up to and including full sun. Southern windows preferred. Note than many orchids do not like the hot, drying direct-afternoon sun of western windows.

Under lights: Four fluorescent 4 ft. (1.2 m) long tubes, preferably full-spectrum, about 6 in. (15 cm) above the leaves.

Temperature

There are also three standard categories of temperature for classifying orchids, with more emphasis on minimum night temperatures than on day. Note this especially: for best blooming, orchids prefer at least a 10°F (5°C) drop in temperature at night, and many orchids do not perform well in temperatures above 85°F (29°C).

Warm: Very comfortable room temperature days, 68°F (20°C) or higher, nights not below 60°F (16°C).

Intermediate: Room temperature days, 60°F (16°C) or higher, nights between 50–60°F (10–16°C).

Cool: Room temperature days, 55°F (13°C) or higher, nights between 40–50°F (4–10°C).

Fertilizer

Orchids generally need far less fertilizer than other plants. Remember that life in a tree only gives access to small amounts of nutrients, although these small amounts often are available on a frequent basis. Therefore, the general advice is to fertilize your orchids "weakly, weekly." Get a fertilizer especially made for orchids, a kind that can be dissolved in water and applied. I advise always using a general orchid fertilizer rather than one formulated as a "bloom booster." Note that some orchid potting mix is sold with fertilizer already in it; this tends to be a finer-sized mix better suited for terrestrials (*Cymbidium*, *Paphiopedilum*) than for those that need coarser bark (such as *Cattleya*).

Plant Size

For simplicity, I've used three size categories so you can anticipate how large an orchid can get. I also sometimes use the term "compact" to indicate a plant of a manageable size that produces its flowers relatively close to the leaves, or one whose foliage stays short even if wide.

Small: under 10 in. (25 cm) tall.

Medium: 10–17 in. (25–43 cm) tall.

Large: 18 in. (46 cm) or taller.

Hybrid Crosses

Orchids have millions of seeds in each seed pod, which means that even within a single interbreeding of two parents (a *hybrid cross*), there are millions of possible DNA combinations, and the progeny can look wildly different. That's why there are so many different *cultivars* (which specifies an exact orchid) in every single orchid hybrid cross. To obtain an exact copy, you must buy a *meristem* (or *mericlone*, often used interchangeably, which is a laboratory-made copy). In the case of plants that can't be cloned via laboratory conditions, in order to get an exact copy, you must buy a *division* (or piece) of an actual plant. Names of exact copies of specific plants will be set off by single quotation marks, for example, *Beallara* Peggy Ruth Carpenter 'Morning Joy'. In this example, *Beallara* is the orchid genus, Peggy Ruth Carpenter is the hybrid cross, and 'Morning Joy' is a specific, exact plant whose flowers will look the same no matter where you buy it.

Awards

Orchid cultivar names often have letters after them, indicating that the plant has won an award. These letters actually become part of the official name of the orchid. The American Orchid Society (AOS) and the Royal Horticultural Society (RHS), among other organizations, bestow orchid flower awards in various grades. Highest is the FCC (First Class Certificate); next is the AM (Award of Merit);

third is the HCC (Highly Commended Certificate). So, for example, FCC/AOS means the plant was awarded a First Class Certificate from the American Orchid Society for outstanding flower quality.

Name Confusion

You will note that some orchids are known by several different scientific names. There's been a lot of taxonomic rearranging of species, and the Royal Horticultural Society, which does the official orchid hybrid record-keeping, has updated its database to reflect many of these changes. This has caused confusion that will settle eventually. In the meantime, be prepared for some bewildering back-and-forthing.

To make it as easy as possible for you to navigate the finding and buying of plants, I've organized this book by the most commonly used botanical names (even if technically incorrect), as well as providing the taxonomically correct ones. In each hybrid plant entry, the line "Parentage" will contain the taxonomically correct genus for both parents as well as for the hybrid cross.

And, here's a general trick in pronouncing Latin- and Greek-derived orchid names: as far as possible, pronounce every letter.

10 Best Tips for Growing Orchids

1. **Buy** a healthy-looking plant in bloom each month for a year. That way, you'll always have a calendar full of flowers, since many orchids rebloom the same time each year. When buying orchids not in flower, get the biggest, healthiest-looking, unshriveled plant you can afford; tiny and/or stressed ones are probably years away from flowering.

2. Make sure plants have enough of the right **light**. Rule of thumb: leaves should be grassy green rather than dark green or bleached out. *An orchid can grow in light too low for flowering, but it certainly won't bloom there.* And blooms are the whole point!

3. **Water** about once a week, in the morning, *thoroughly and copiously*, at the sink, letting water drain through the pot completely. Rule of thumb: let the mix dry out an inch (about 2 cm) down before watering again. Pots must have at least one hole, and *orchids should never stand in water*. Otherwise, the roots will rot. In winter, reduce watering slightly, when plants often rest.

4. **Fertilize** plants weekly with water-soluble, general orchid fertilizer. If that's too often to remember, do it once a month. Most orchids don't need excessive fertilizer. Flush out the pots with plain water once a month to get rid of accumulated fertilizer salts.

5. **Drop the night temperature** by at least 10°F (5°C) for several weeks, especially in fall, to trigger blooms. This will happen naturally if you summer orchids outdoors until autumn. *If your orchid is in the right light, but never blooms, the lack of a temperature drop at night is probably the problem.*

6. **Summer plants outdoors**, in dappled indirect sunlight. Move them gradually into higher light to avoid sunburn. Fresh air, rainwater, and natural light really give orchids a boost. Let them stay outside until night temperatures fall to 50°F (10°C).

7. **Grow** plants together on a large tray of pebbles that's filled with water (but not so pots sit in water). Groupings and pebble trays help raise the humidity, which orchids love. Keep plants away from hot radiators and cold air conditioners; both are very drying. Give orchids a fan instead.

8. Immediately **repot** new orchids that are in tiny pots into bigger ones with fresh orchid mix, as well as plants that are in old, broken-down mix. Use high-quality mix to avoid having to repot often. Pre-soak the new mix in warm water for an hour before use. Repot every year or two when you start to see new roots and beginnings of new growth; usually this is after bloom, or in spring.

9. **Do pest control**. Periodically look underneath leaves and in plant crevices for signs of insects such as little brown scales, translucent green aphids, white cottony masses of mealybug, silvering of leaves caused by thrips, or flying whiteflies. Use houseplant insecticidal soap several times a few days apart to eliminate them, dousing the plant all over and under leaves, soaking into the pot.

10. **Give up** on and give away those orchids that just don't do well for you. No matter how easy a plant might be for most people, if your conditions aren't right for it, it's just not worth the time and trouble. Buy a different type of orchid instead.

(left) When repotting your orchid, make sure that it's at the proper level. The monopodial *Phalaenopsis* on the left is seated properly, while the right one is seated too high in the pot, allowing roots to dry out too much.

(right) Spray an infested orchid plant completely with insecticidal soap especially made for houseplants, under and above leaves, so that the spray drips.

Tolumnia

Angraecum

Big Phalaenopsis

The Plants

Splash Petal Cattleya

Belleara

Aliceara Sunday Best

Sunday Best Intergeneric Orchid

PRONOUNCED
al-iss-ee-AR-ah

ABBREVIATED
Alcra.

ALSO KNOWN AS
Miltassia (Mtssa.) Sunday Best

THE PLANT
Medium-sized sympodial epiphyte; short flat pseudobulb, grassy leaves, multiple sprays of red-brown blooms

LIGHT NEEDS
Medium; indirect eastern window

TEMPERATURE RANGE
Intermediate; days 70–85°F (21–29°C), winter nights 60–65°F (16–18°C)

POTTING NEEDS
Medium to fine orchid mix, plastic pot

BLOOM TIME
Anytime

Aliceara Sunday Best
Orchid checklist:

✓ Grows on sunny windowsill
✓ Long-lasting flowers
✓ Sprays of multiple flowers
✓ Big flowers
  Great cut flower
✓ Intensely colored or patterned
✓ Noted for fragrance
✓ Attractive plant habit
✓ Once-a-week watering and fertilizer
✓ Repeat bloom
  Grows under fluorescent lights
✓ Grows easily into specimen

Orchids have an amazing ability to interbreed among different groups (known as genera), especially when humans get busy with a pollinating toothpick. The result is called an *intergeneric* orchid. The intergeneric *Aliceara* combines the best of Spider Orchid (*Brassia*), Pansy Orchid (*Miltonia*), and Dancing Lady Orchid (*Oncidium*). A bit of trivia: anytime you see "ara" at the end of an orchid genus, it means at least three genera are in the DNA.

Such jumbling creates plants with great hybrid vigor. *Aliceara* Sunday Best is a free-flowering compact hybrid with long-petalled flowers that look like they're jumping for joy. The cultivar 'Ontario' has a big, long, prettily patterned fuchsia lip coupled with mahogany striped petals and sepals—it reminds me of a cosmic explosion. The 5 in. (13 cm) long blooms, six to eight on each spike above bright green grassy leaves, are subtly fragrant.

Another lovely cultivar is 'Muffin'. It's paler with a dusty rose lip that develops a wonderful greenish edge with age. Flowers are beautifully presented on the stem.

Note that sometimes Sunday Best is mislabeled *Miltassia* rather than *Aliceara*.

Easy to grow, Sunday Best does well in average room temperatures, on any bright window sheltered from direct sun. The light is right if leaves are grassy green; they're reddish when it's too high, dark green if insufficient. Water often enough that new growths don't shrivel. Repot every two years.

Sunday Best will flower when it reaches about a foot in height. Treat it to a 10°F (5°C) drop at night to trigger blooms.

So it's not a natural beauty. The man-made Sunday Best is still a head-turner.

PARENTAGE: *Aliceara* Sunday Best (*Brassidium* Gilded Urchin × *Miltonia spectabilis*)

Hybrid vigor comes from mixing different types of orchids together, resulting in easier-to-grow, freer flowering plants such as *Aliceara* Sunday Best 'Muffin', HCC/AOS (right), and the much darker and very different Sunday Best 'Ontario', HCC/AOS (page 8, third from top).

Angraecum leonis
Lion's Moustache Orchid

PRONOUNCED
an-GRAY-cum lee-OH-nis

ABBREVIATED
Angcm.

THE PLANT
Small monopodial epiphyte; arching fanlike fleshy leaves, starry white fragrant flowers

LIGHT NEEDS
Low to medium; any window but northern, under lights; adaptable

TEMPERATURE RANGE
Warm; days 70–90°F (21–32°C), winter nights 65–70°F (18–21°C)

POTTING NEEDS
Medium to coarse orchid bark, small plastic or clay pot

BLOOM TIME
Can be anytime; peak February to May

Angraecum leonis
Orchid checklist:

✓ **Grows on sunny windowsill**
✓ **Long-lasting flowers**
✓ **Sprays of multiple flowers**
✓ **Big flowers**
  Great cut flower
  Intensely colored or patterned
✓ **Noted for fragrance**
✓ **Attractive plant habit**
✓ **Once-a-week watering and fertilizer**
  Repeat bloom
✓ **Grows under fluorescent lights**
✓ **Grows easily into specimen**

Angraecum leonis is known as the Lion's Mustache Orchid, but frankly, I can't see a cat's maw in there. That complaint aside, this is one of the first orchids I grew, blooming it reliably under lights. I love the long-spurred, pristine white flowers that sparkle as if with fairy dust. And their fragrance is of jasmine, incredibly strong at night, amazing on such a little plant.

This is my idea of a perfect combination between plant and flowers, like a song where music and lyrics are really well matched. The succulent 1 in. (2.5 cm) wide bright green leaves arch in pretty, alternating fashion, so that the plant is usually less than 8 in. (20 cm) wide, 6 in. (15 cm) high, and the starry big-lipped flowers, about 3 in. (8 cm) long, are displayed against the foliage like white decorations on a fan. There can be a half-dozen per flower spike at a time, but even when there's only one, it's still a lovely six-week effect.

The species is found only on Madagascar and nearby Comoro Island off Africa. The Comoran type has bigger flowers and is more vigorous. Either one is wonderful.

Grow *Angraecum leonis* warm, in as small a pot that will hold the roots, in fast-draining mix, and water well when actively growing, allowing the mix to dry an inch (2.5 cm) in between, and fertilize weekly. The fleshy leaves should never shrivel. Cut back water and fertilizer a bit in autumn. It resents salts, so flush the pots with rainwater once a month.

Lionlike or not, this is a great little orchid, with a big roar.

The genus *Angraecum* was made famous by Charles Darwin, who saw the long nectar spurs and predicted there must be a very long-tongued moth pollinator. It took fifty years to prove him right. *Angraecum leonis* is shown here and on page 25 (top left).

Ascocenda Hybrids

Intergeneric Vanda Orchid

PRONOUNCED
az-koe-SEN-dah

ABBREVIATED
Ascda.

THE PLANT
Medium-sized monopodial epiphyte; coarse aerial roots, flat, alternating straplike leaves, sturdy stem of vibrant flowers

LIGHT NEEDS
High; southern window

TEMPERATURE RANGE
Warm; days 65–95°F (18–35°C), winter nights 60–65°F (16–18°C)

POTTING NEEDS
Coarse orchid bark or no mix, clay pot or hanging basket

BLOOM TIME
Anytime, two or three times a year

Ascocenda Hybrids
Orchid checklist:

✓ Grows on sunny windowsill
✓ Long-lasting flowers
✓ Sprays of multiple flowers
✓ Big flowers
✓ Great cut flower
✓ Intensely colored or patterned
  Noted for fragrance
✓ Attractive plant habit
  Once-a-week watering and fertilizer
✓ Repeat bloom
  Grows under fluorescent lights
✓ Grows easily into specimen

Some of the most brilliantly colored orchids on earth bloom on the sun-worshipping hybrids between compact *Ascocentrum* and tall *Vanda*. Every so often I see an *Ascocenda* that looks washed-out, but the majority of them have stunning strong color and sometimes intense spotting. The numerous big, round, flat flowers, held on strong stems, range from red, orange, peach, yellow, fuchsia, purple, and even blue. The long-lasting flowers can appear several times a year.

Ascocenda likes to be warm, and thrive in southern sunny parts of the country where people complain, "It's not the heat, it's the humidity." Even if you live in less tropical-like areas, give your *Ascocenda* as much light as possible, water daily in the morning, provide weekly orchid fertilizer, and grow it with lots of other plants, which helps bump up humidity.

Since *Ascocenda* is similar to *Vanda*, it is grown the same way, but tends to be much more compact. Since they're not so gangly in plant habit, ascocendas are easier to manage. Given a choice between the two, choose *Ascocenda*.

Insects and disease are uncommon; usually you'll only see bugs if humidity is low, causing stress. Summer plants outdoors, moving them gradually, over a few days, into the highest light so the leaves won't blacken and burn. They may need daily water. Fertilize weekly for abundant bloom.

Ascocendas don't like to be repotted. If the mix deteriorates, just dig it out and add more, or if the plant is in a wooden basket with no mix, just put the entire basket into a bigger one.

Brilliant color and repeat blooming are highlights of sun-loving *Ascocenda* hybrids like Fuchs Baby Doll (right), Brighton Fuchsia (left), and Orange Sparkler (page 9, top).

Baptistonia echinata

Bumblebee Orchid

PRONOUNCED
bap-tees-TONE-ee-ah eck-in-AY-tah

ABBREVIATED
Bapt.

THE PLANT
Small sympodial epiphyte; long pseudobulb, two stiff glossy leaves, long spike of multiple little yellow-and-maroon blooms

LIGHT NEEDS
Medium; indirect southern or western window, under lights

TEMPERATURE RANGE
Warm to intermediate; days 60–95°F (16–35°C), winter nights 60–70°F (16–21°C); very adaptable

POTTING NEEDS
Medium orchid mix, small clay pot

BLOOM TIME
February to May, can repeat in fall

Baptistonia echinata
Orchid checklist:

✓ Grows on sunny windowsill
✓ Long-lasting flowers
✓ Sprays of multiple flowers
  Big flowers
  Great cut flower
✓ Intensely colored or patterned
  Noted for fragrance
✓ Attractive plant habit
  Once-a-week watering and fertilizer
✓ Repeat bloom
✓ Grows under fluorescent lights
✓ Grows easily into specimen

Some orchids are simply darling. There's just no other word for them. In this isn't-that-adorable category belongs the diminutive Bumblebee Orchid, *Baptistonia echinata*. If this easygoing little sweetie doesn't steal your heart, nothing will.

Native to Brazil, the Bumblebee Orchid is aptly named—the spray of vibrant yellow and dark reddish brown blooms makes you think it's covered in a swarm of bees. Looking more closely, each 1 in. (2.5 cm) wide flower even seems to possess barred little wings. It clearly aims to attract a bee pollinator, who tries to "mate" with this deceptive little mimic.

Related to yellow Dancing Lady *Oncidium*, *Baptistonia echinata* can have dozens of flowers on a pendant spike that emerges from the bottom of the growth. The plant blooms young, in pots as small as 2.5 in. (6.4 cm), and as it gets older, there can be multiple-branched spikes that reach 2 ft. (0.6 m) long, full of bees at the ends.

Exceptionally easy, Bumblebee does best in bright indirect light, even blooming under fluorescent tubes. It's incredibly temperature-tolerant, but drop the temperature somewhat at night. As with many orchids, it responds to high humidity, so stand the pot on a water-filled tray of pebbles, so it's above, not in, the water. Water often while growing, letting it dry just slightly in between, and fertilize weekly. Once the growth is mature, stop fertilizing and reduce watering a bit to give the plant a short rest, resuming once flower spikes appear. Repot it into fresh mix annually, after bloom.

You'll swear you hear buzzing.

Baptistonia echinata is a charming, compact species that can grow quickly into a specimen bearing hundreds of little bumblebee-like blooms.

Beallara Peggy Ruth Carpenter

Peggy Ruth Carpenter Intergeneric Orchid

PRONOUNCED
bee-al-AR-ah

ABBREVIATED
Bllra.

THE PLANT
Medium-sized sympodial epiphyte; long narrow pseudobulb, grassy leaves, sprays of starry big blooms

LIGHT NEEDS
Medium; bright indirect eastern or southern window

TEMPERATURE RANGE
Intermediate; days 65–75°F (18–24°C), winter nights 55–60°F (13–16°C)

POTTING NEEDS
Fine orchid mix, small plastic pot

BLOOM TIME
Winter to spring, can repeat in summer

Beallara Peggy Ruth Carpenter Orchid checklist:

✓ Grows on sunny windowsill
✓ Long-lasting flowers
✓ Sprays of multiple flowers
✓ Big flowers
　Great cut flower
✓ Intensely colored or patterned
✓ Noted for fragrance
✓ Attractive plant habit
　Once-a-week watering and fertilizer
✓ Repeat bloom
　Grows under fluorescent lights
✓ Grows easily into specimen

If you need proof that orchids are in an active state of evolution, witness their readiness to let hybridizers mix their DNA to create new genera. Over time, humans have interbred at least nine related orchid groups together to create a single orchid hybrid. It's bewildering to keep up with what's mixed with what. The hybrid genus *Beallara* is still manageable, for this intergeneric *only* has four different Oncidium groups within it.

Of the many lovely *Beallara* crosses, Peggy Ruth Carpenter is my favorite, especially the elegant, popular cultivar 'Morning Joy'. The starry 4.5 in. (11 cm) long pink-flushed blooms have lavender tinges, light purple blotches, and long white lips marked in red and lavender.

Here's an example of great variety within a cross: the awarded cultivar Peggy Ruth Carpenter 'J. E. M.', AM/AOS, is completely different than 'Morning Joy'. It's purple with dark purple leopard spots, has a more vivid, waterfall-patterned frilly lip, and fuller flower form.

Peggy Ruth Carpenter grows quickly, often with several 10 in. (25 cm) branching spikes blooming in small pots. Flowers are lightly fragrant of spice.

This hybrid has a lot of Pansy Orchid (*Miltonia*) heritage, giving it that amazing lip and compact habit. The other influences are Spider Orchid (*Brassia*), Snail Shell Orchid (*Cochlioda*), and Toothed Tongue Orchid (*Odontoglossum*).

When people have trouble with Peggy Ruth Carpenter, it's usually because the humidity is low. Keep it from drying out completely, in bright indirect sun, away from extreme heat. Fertilize every other week, and repot after bloom when new growth starts crawling over the edge.

PARENTAGE: *Beallara* Peggy Ruth Carpenter (Tahoma Glacier × *Miltonia* Purple Queen)

Gorgeous pastel colors and lovely markings make *Beallara* Peggy Ruth Carpenter 'Morning Joy' (right) a highly coveted cultivar of this extremely popular quad-generic cross. A completely different look is found in the dark cultivar 'J.E.M.', AM/AOS (page 25, bottom right), demonstrating how much a hybrid cross can vary.

Brassada Orange Delight

Orange Delight Intergeneric Spider Orchid

PRONOUNCED
brass-AY-dah

ABBREVIATED
Brsa.

THE PLANT
Compact sympodial epiphyte;
flattish pseudobulb, wide grassy
leaves, orange spidery blooms

LIGHT NEEDS
Medium; eastern window

TEMPERATURE RANGE
Intermediate; days 65–85°F
(18–29°C), winter nights 55–65°F
(13–18°C); tolerant

POTTING NEEDS
Medium orchid mix, plastic pot

BLOOM TIME
Generally autumn, often repeats
in spring

**Brassada Orange Delight
Orchid checklist:**

✓ Grows on sunny windowsill
✓ Long-lasting flowers
✓ Sprays of multiple flowers
✓ Big flowers
  Great cut flower
✓ Noted for fragrance
✓ Attractive plant habit
  Once-a-week watering and fertilizer
✓ Repeat bloom
✓ Grows under fluorescent lights
✓ Grows easily into specimen

Few orchids combine such a rich orange palette with a long-legged spidery look to the flowers, and Orange Delight does it best. It's a unique man-made hybrid between the intensely orange, odd flowers of the Red-Orange Ada (*Ada aurantiaca*), and an easy, free-flowering Spider Orchid hybrid (*Brassia*), both from South America. The result gives intriguing sprays of brilliant 2.5 in. (6.4 cm) orange blooms, doing five to twenty-five jumping jacks in a row.

Both parents are fragrant, and so is Orange Delight. The delightful scent reminds me of honey and cinnamon on grapefruit, and gets stronger with age. The strong color also deepens, from a clear vibrant orange to rich autumnal tones.

'Starbek' and the similar 'Starbek Orange' are the cultivars most often sold, both awarded varieties with long, ruffled yellowish lips, long "legs" that curve out at the edges like the flower is wearing elfin shoes, and just enough brown splotches to give a rakish air.

Orange Delight often sends up two flower spikes per growth. The hybrid vigor also makes it bloom while very young, and it is easy to flower twice a year.

The plant is compact, under 1 ft. (30 cm) high, and fits nicely on an eastern window, protected from hot rays. It's fairly temperature-tolerant. Water it weekly, so that it dries only slightly in between, and fertilize every other week. I find it likes fresh potting mix, so repot annually after blooming in spring or summer. When Orange Delight sulks, it's usually because it's too hot, or the potting mix is old and sour.

PARENTAGE: *Brassada* Orange Delight (*Ada aurantiaca* × *Brassia* Mary Traub Levin)

Brassada Orange Delight 'Starbek', HCC/AOS, is the most common variety, and its color deepens as the long-lasting flowers age.

Brassavola nodosa and Hybrids
Lady-of-the-Night Orchid

PRONOUNCED
bra-sah-VOH-lah no-DOH-sah

ABBREVIATED
B.

THE PLANT
Compact sympodial epiphyte; slender stem, single leaf, one to six fragrant starry white and green big-lipped flowers

LIGHT NEEDS
Medium to high; southern window

TEMPERATURE RANGE
Warm; days 70–85°F (21–29°C), winter nights 60°F (16°C) or higher, adaptable

POTTING NEEDS
Medium to large orchid bark, plastic pot just big enough to hold roots

BLOOM TIME
Anytime, peak in autumn

Brassavola nodosa and Hybrids Orchid checklist:

✓ Grows on sunny windowsill
✓ Long-lasting flowers
✓ Sprays of multiple flowers
✓ Big flowers
  Great cut flower
  Intensely colored or patterned
✓ Noted for fragrance
✓ Attractive plant habit
  Once-a-week watering and fertilizer
✓ Repeat bloom
  Grows under fluorescent lights
✓ Grows easily into specimen

While many orchids wow with color, others charm with subtler seduction. The green and white Lady-of-the-Night captured my heart one evening when I caught the wonderful fragrance of something like freesia and orange blossoms in the air. When I went searching, I found the perfume emanating from the 4 in. (10 cm) long, starry, big-lipped flowers of this charming, compact plant. Native from Mexico to Venezuela, *Brassavola nodosa* can be ever-blooming, peaking in fall when most other orchids are flowerless. It's a must in any easy collection.

Exceptionally adaptable, *Brassavola nodosa* does best with warm days and the medium-bright light of a southern window, watered twice weekly, and fertilized once a week. If it's not flowering in early September, hold back water for a few weeks; that often helps to trigger blooms. It tends not to flower if too cold at night.

A word to the wise: I've stuck my nose now into many different Lady-of-the-Night blooms over the years, and fragrance can be wildly variable, from intense to non-existent. If fragrance is the key to your heart, get a meristem (exact copy) that is stated to be fragrant. Or else buy one in bloom that is well-scented, but choose at night, since that's when the fragrance kicks in, a lure for their night-flying moth pollinators. Perfume begins at sunset, and peaks at midnight.

When used as a parent, *Brassavola nodosa* can create adorable offspring that are fragrant, but, again, scent can vary. I highly recommend the hybrid *Brassavola* Little Stars (*nodosa* × *subulifolia*), which really increases the flower count.

The hybrid *Brassavola* Little Stars (right) lends more flowers to the fragrant display of Lady-of-the-Night orchids, but the simple beauty of the species *Brassavola nodosa* (left) makes it also worth growing.

Brassia

Spider Orchid

PRONOUNCED
BRASS-ee-ah

ABBREVIATED
Brs.

THE PLANT
Medium to large sympodial epiphyte; oval pseudobulb, grassy strap leaves, starry flowers with long sepals and petals

LIGHT NEEDS
Medium; any window but northern

TEMPERATURE RANGE
Intermediate to warm; days 60–85°F (16–29°C), winter nights 55–65°F (13–18°C)

POTTING NEEDS
Medium orchid mix, plastic or clay pot or basket

BLOOM TIME
Spring to summer; may repeat

Brassia
Orchid checklist:

✓ **Grows on sunny windowsill**
✓ **Long-lasting flowers**
✓ **Sprays of multiple flowers**
✓ **Big flowers**
  Great cut flower
✓ **Intensely colored or patterned**
✓ **Noted for fragrance**
✓ **Attractive plant habit**
  Once-a-week watering and fertilizer
✓ **Repeat bloom**
  Grows under fluorescent lights
✓ **Grows easily into specimen**

If you are looking for spectacular orchid flowers, search no further than the astonishing Spider Orchids. These tropical Americans boast blooms up to 10 in. (25 cm) long, with thin petals and sepals that elongate into even narrower points. They do look like spiders. No wonder. They're trying to attract the spider-eating wasps that pollinate them.

Spider Orchids are often perfumed, with ten to twenty arranged like Rockettes on a spike. While their shape is jaw-dropping, the colors are more boring: yellow-green and brown predominate. That's why brilliantly toned intergeneric hybrids are more popular, although Brassias themselves are still well worth growing.

Brassias make up the heart of many intergeneric hybrids in the Oncidium group, because they are so easy to grow, while also bestowing big flowers with the fabulous spidery look to their offspring. (See *Aliceara, Beallara, Brassada, Brassidium, Degarmoara, Miltassia.*)

Of hybrids within *Brassia* itself, a famous one is *Brassia* Rex (*verrucosa × gireoudiana*), whose white-lipped green flowers can grow an amazing *foot (30 cm)* long. The buds look like little green peppers.

Grow *Brassia* in slightly less light than for *Cattleya* types. Morning sun is great; leaves will be yellowish green in the best light. It prefers not to dry out. Water in the morning to keep the tightly clustered pseudobulbs from rotting. Fertilizer encourages twice-a-year blooms, so feed every two weeks when it's actively growing. When the growth is mature, stop fertilizing and let the plant rest for a couple of weeks, reducing water somewhat. Repot after bloom, only when really necessary.

See? Spiders aren't so yucky after all.

Brassias are some of the easiest orchids to grow, with daddy longlegs spidery flowers. Shown here is *Brassia* Rex. The species *Brassia maculata* is pictured on page 6 (bottom).

Brassidium Kenneth Bivin

Kenneth Bivin Intergeneric Spider Orchid

PRONOUNCED
brass-SID-ee-um

ABBREVIATED
Brsdm.

ALSO KNOWN AS
Odontobrassia (*Odbrs.*) Kenneth
Bivin

THE PLANT
Medium-sized sympodial epiphyte;
flattish pseudobulb, leathery leaves,
very long spike of spidery flowers

LIGHT NEEDS
Medium to high; southern window

TEMPERATURE RANGE
Intermediate; days 60–80°F
(16–27°C), winter nights 50–60°F
(10–16°C); tolerant

POTTING NEEDS
Medium orchid mix, plastic pot

BLOOM TIME
Anytime

**Brassidium Kenneth Bivin
Orchid checklist:**

✓ Grows on sunny windowsill
✓ Long-lasting flowers
✓ Sprays of multiple flowers
✓ Big flowers
✓ Great cut flower
✓ Intensely colored or patterned
✓ Noted for fragrance
✓ Attractive plant habit
✓ Once-a-week watering and fertilizer
✓ Repeat bloom
  Grows under fluorescent lights
✓ Grows easily into specimen

I always smile when I see *Brassidium* Kenneth Bivin in bloom. The flowers look like they are white-skirted cheerleaders, caught halfway through doing the splits.

This is another in the line of vigorous, free-flowering Spider Orchid intergenerics, this time using the green and brown Arching Spider Orchid (*Brassia arcuigera*), and adding the red, yellow and white Keeled *Oncidium cariniferum*. The floral results are often 4 in. (10 cm) wide, dark mahogany red with curly yellow tips and white lips, borne a dozen or more on a spike up to 4 ft. (1.2 m) long. The foliage and flower stem can be a bit curly too. Even the buds are pretty.

Kenneth Bivin flowers anytime, and big plants can be in bloom constantly. The long-lasting flowers have a sweet, intense, cedar fragrance.

Brassidium hybrids in general are tolerant and easy to bloom, so if you see other types available, the same basic culture will apply. Give them bright light, room temperatures, water so they dry out at least an inch down between times, and fertilize weekly. Cut off the spikes when they finish blooming.

There is often confusion in the name when you go to buy the Kenneth Bivin intergeneric hybrid, because its *Oncidium* parent used to be classified as an *Odontoglossum*, making this technically now a *Brassidium* instead of the old (but often still used) *Odontobrassia*. Also, Kenneth Bivin seems to be spelled a hundred different ways (Bivens, Biven, Blivin, Bevins, Keneth, Kevin …). I checked, and Kenneth Bivin is correct. Under whatever moniker you find it, give in to temptation and scoop it up for your own.

PARENTAGE: *Brassidium* Kenneth Bivin (*Oncidium cariniferum* × *Brassia arcuigera*)

Brassidium Kenneth Bivin 'Santa Barbara', AM/AOS, is an award-winning beauty.

Brassolaeliocattleya Ports of Paradise
Ports of Paradise Cattleya

PRONOUNCED
brass-oh-lay-lee-oh-KAT-lee-ah

ABBREVIATED
Blc.

CORRECTLY KNOWN AS
Rhynchosophrocattleya (*Rsc.*) Ports of Paradise

THE PLANT
Large sympodial epiphyte; long stemlike pseudobulb, single stiff leaf, huge fragrant green blooms

LIGHT NEEDS
Medium to high; southern window, protected from hottest rays

TEMPERATURE RANGE
Intermediate; days 65–85°F (18–29°C), winter nights 55–60°F (13–16°C)

POTTING NEEDS
Medium orchid bark, small clay or plastic pot

BLOOM TIME
Peak summer to fall

***Brassolaeliocattleya* Ports of Paradise Orchid checklist:**

✓ Grows on sunny windowsill
✓ Long-lasting flowers
✓ Sprays of multiple flowers
✓ Big flowers
✓ Great cut flower
✓ Noted for fragrance
✓ Attractive plant habit
✓ Once-a-week watering and fertilizer
✓ Repeat bloom
  Grows under fluorescent lights
✓ Grows easily into specimen

Ports of Paradise is, quite simply, an orchid classic. First hybridized in 1970, few other *Cattleya* types have had its staying power. It's impossible not to love it.

This is an enormous flower, in gorgeous chartreuse-green that fades into yellow, with a beautifully frilled, flared, and fimbriated lip. The 6 in. (15 cm) blooms—usually two or three per spike—have exceptional substance, held strongly above the leaves. Once mature, it can bloom twice yearly.

Those wonderful qualities would be enough to admire this hybrid excessively. Add to all that the real wow factor: incredible fragrance. Fragrance that takes your breath away and that completely befits a green flower: intense tart lemon, mixed with lily-of-the-valley. It gets even stronger in the evening.

The scent and the fringed lip come from its famous parent, *Rhyncolaelia digbyana*, a Mexican/Central American species. Warning: herein lies a messy name confusion. *Rhyncholaelia digbyana* used to be called *Brassavola digbyana*, making Ports of Paradise a *Brassolaeliocattleya*. Then taxonomists moved *Brassavola digbyana* into *Rhyncholaelia* instead. They also moved Port's *Laelia* ancestor into *Sophronitis*. So P-of-P is technically a *Rhynchosophrocattleya*. Sigh. You'll usually find it still labeled *Blc.* (*Brassolaeliocattleya*), but not always. I apologize. I don't make this stuff up just to drive you crazy.

Grow this fabulous hybrid in fairly high light, a bit more than for most *Cattleya* types. I've noticed it tends to bloom more readily if pot-bound, so let it sit a couple of years before repotting into a not-overly-large pot.

Meristems (exact copies) of some of the best cultivars are readily available.

PARENTAGE: *Rhynchosophrocattleya* Ports of Paradise (Fortune × *Rhyncholaelia digbyana*)

Huge flowers and intense fragrance help make *Brassolaeliocattleya* Ports of Paradise a showstopper. 'Emerald Isle', FCC/AOS (top), is one of the most famous and awarded *Brassolaeliocattleya* cultivars available. Pictured below it is the cultivar 'Green Ching Hua', AM/AOS.

Burrageara Nelly Isler

Nelly Isler Intergeneric Orchid

PRONOUNCED
bur-ra-JER-ah

ABBREVIATED
Burr.

THE PLANT
Compact sympodial epiphyte; flat-tish pseudobulb, grassy leaves, long spike of red flowers

LIGHT NEEDS
Medium; eastern or southern window protected from direct sun, under lights

TEMPERATURE RANGE
Intermediate to warm; days 60–80°F (16–27°C), winter nights 55–60°F (13–16°C); tolerant

POTTING NEEDS
Sphagnum moss or fine orchid mix, plastic pot

BLOOM TIME
Two or three times a year

Burrageara Nelly Isler
Orchid checklist:

✓ Grows on sunny windowsill
✓ Long-lasting flowers
✓ Sprays of multiple flowers
✓ Big flowers
  Great cut flower
✓ Intensely colored or patterned
✓ Noted for fragrance
✓ Attractive plant habit
✓ Once-a-week watering and fertilizer
✓ Repeat bloom
✓ Grows under fluorescent lights
✓ Grows easily into specimen

It never ceases to amaze me how readily orchids will inter-breed among different, if related, genera. A case in point: the man-made genus of *Burrageara*, which combines four genera from the tropical Americas: *Cochlioda* × *Miltonia* × *Odontoglossum* × *Oncidium*. Such mixes lend tolerant hybrid vigor and additional flowering times.

Nelly Isler has a bit more Pansy Orchid (*Miltonia*) and Snail Shell Orchid (*Cochlioda*) in it than the other two parental influences, which gives a neat, grassy-leaved plant habit, and really pumps up the neon-red coloration in the 3 in. (8 cm) long flowers. The fabulous pansy lip is big and decorative, with a vibrant yellow "eye" at the center of the bloom.

Fragrance is another enticing feature. The scent intensifies over the first few days, a mix of spice and citrus.

Grow Nelly Isler in bright light, but shield the leaves from the hottest direct sun, because they can sunburn and blacken. Leaves speckle when they are at the top end of the light range. Give it a 10°F (5°C) drop in night temperature to stimulate budding.

Line the top of the pot with sphagnum moss (or use moss entirely as the potting mix), and when the moss is dry at the top, water. If you have any trouble with the plant, try using rainwater instead of tap, and increase humidity. Don't let new growths shrivel, although older ones invariably will. Repot every two years. Fertilize twice a month, and multiple blooms may appear almost anytime.

Burrageara honors Albert Burrage, first president of the American Orchid Society.

PARENTAGE: *Burrageara* Nelly Isler (Stefan Isler × *Miltonia* Kensington)

The intergeneric Nelly Isler is a lovely, grassy-leaved plant bearing intense red blooms.

(inset) One of the parents of Nelly Isler is *Burrageara* Stefan Isler (*Vuylstekeara* Edna × *Oncidium leucochilum*), a somewhat larger plant that is also very popular and easy to grow. Shown here is the cultivar 'Lava Flow'.

Cattleya aurantiaca

Orange Cattleya

PRONOUNCED
KAT-lee-ah aw-ran-tee-AH-kah

ABBREVIATED
C.

CORRECTLY KNOWN AS
Guarianthe (*G.* or *Gur.*) *aurantiaca*

THE PLANT
Large sympodial epiphyte; long stemlike pseudobulb, two stiff leaves, clusters of small orange or yellow flowers

LIGHT NEEDS
Medium; any window but northern

TEMPERATURE RANGE
Intermediate to warm; days 65–85°F (18–29°C), winter nights 55–65°F (13–18°C)

POTTING NEEDS
Medium orchid mix, plastic or clay pot

BLOOM TIME
Late winter to spring

Cattleya aurantiaca
Orchid checklist:

✓ **Grows on sunny windowsill**
✓ **Long-lasting flowers**
✓ **Sprays of multiple flowers**
  Big flowers
✓ **Great cut flower**
✓ **Intensely colored or patterned**
  Noted for fragrance
✓ **Attractive plant habit**
✓ **Once-a-week watering and fertilizer**
✓ **Repeat bloom**
  Grows under fluorescent lights
✓ **Grows easily into specimen**

While *Cattleya*-type orchid hybrids are easiest to buy, sometimes it's great to go back to a classic species that is the source of many intense colors in those hybrids. *Cattleya aurantiaca*, now formally reclassified into a new genus called *Guarianthe*, is one of those great, simple classics. Its orange is spectacular, truly neon. The yellow form will also knock your socks off.

It is tall and gangly; at nearly 2 ft. (0.6 m) it will likely be your tallest *Cattleya*. It will only bloom once a year, although fortunately it starts when still young. But when it's in bloom, everyone—and I mean everyone—will take notice. The many 1.5 to 2 in. (4 to 5 cm) flowers are borne in a cluster that revs up the potency of the colors. Blooms are so shiny and waxy that people touch them and still think they are artificial.

The flowers usually don't open fully, blooming cupped forward, although selections often have open presentations. Either way, the color still reigns.

Very easy to grow, give *Cattleya aurantiaca* any bright exposure in average room temperatures, summer it outside and leave it to get a fall drop in temperature. It will produce multiple sheaths with buds inside. I do warn: you'll feel like you're waiting forever for those buds to emerge from their sheathing. The wait is worth it.

So stick this gawky Mexican species at the back of the window for most of the year. When it blooms, you'll be in awe of what nature does without much help at all.

Often still known as *Cattleya aurantiaca* (right), this tall Mexican species generally comes in brilliant orange or yellow and is correctly called *Guarianthe aurantiaca*. Neon yellow forms like 'Lemon Drop' (left) are a nice change of pace.

Cattleya Chocolate Drop

Chocolate Drop Orchid

PRONOUNCED
KAT-lee-ah

ABBREVIATED
C.

CORRECTLY KNOWN AS
Cattlianthe (Ctt.) Chocolate Drop

THE PLANT
Large sympodial epiphyte; tall pseudobulb, two leathery leaves, cluster of dark waxy blooms

LIGHT NEEDS
Medium; any window but northern

TEMPERATURE RANGE
Intermediate; days 60–85°F (16–29°C), winter nights 55–60°F (13–16°C)

POTTING NEEDS
Medium orchid mix, plastic or clay pot

BLOOM TIME
Fall, can repeat

Cattleya Chocolate Drop Orchid checklist:

✓ Grows on sunny windowsill
✓ Long-lasting flowers
✓ Sprays of multiple flowers
  Big flowers
✓ Great cut flower
✓ Intensely colored or patterned
✓ Noted for fragrance
✓ Attractive plant habit
✓ Once-a-week watering and fertilizer
✓ Repeat bloom
  Grows under fluorescent lights
✓ Grows easily into specimen

Fame comes to some orchids early, and a few wear their notoriety well. The 1965 hybrid Chocolate Drop is so wonderful it deserves its own entry, even though one of its parents, *Cattleya aurantiaca*, also does. It's like *Cattleya aurantiaca* flowers made twice as big, more shapely, even more colorful, and fragrant.

Bearing massive clusters of 3 in. (8 cm) deeply rich coppery red blooms, Chocolate Drop seems carved of wax. The long, distinctive flower lip is two-toned, often yellow and red. Even the buds appear delicious, and do indeed look like Hershey's Kisses.

And, boy, is it fragrant: a sophisticated blend of jasmine and gardenia, with hints of lemony spice. It gets that—and the lip—from its other parent, the spotted Brazilian species *Cattleya guttata*.

The long-lasting flowers will bloom for a couple of months in early autumn, often repeating in winter or spring. Every year, you should have more flowers per cluster.

Easy to grow, Chocolate Drop tolerates neglect bravely, a testament to hybrid vigor. Summer it outdoors, but bring inside before night temperatures drop below 55°F (13°C). Like *Cattleya aurantiaca*, its flower sheaths can develop without buds, and what seems an eternity later, buds usually finally appear. Try not to let water sit on the sheaths.

You may see Chocolate Drop labeled either as *Cattleya*, or the more accurate *Cattlianthe*. Two famous cultivars are the award-winning 'Kodama', AM/AOS, and the newer, wider-petalled 'Volcano Queen'. Both are fabulous.

Chocolate Drop is a tall plant, 18 in. (46 cm) or higher. Bear that in mind when finding room.

PARENTAGE: *Cattlianthe* Chocolate Drop (*Cattleya guttata* × *Guarianthe aurantiaca*)

Clusters of intensely fragrant flowers with thick substance and shining color put *Cattleya* Chocolate Drop on many "all-time-favorite" orchid lists. Shown here is the cultivar 'Kodama', AM/AOS.

Cattleya Group, Splash Petal

Splash Petal Cattleya

PRONOUNCED
KAT-lee-ah

THE PLANT
Compact to large sympodial epiphyte; elongated pseudobulb, one to two leathery leaves, two- or three-toned *Cattleya*-type blooms

LIGHT NEEDS
Medium; any window but northern

TEMPERATURE RANGE
Intermediate; days 65–85°F (18–29°C), winter nights 55–60°F (13–16°C)

POTTING NEEDS
Medium orchid bark, clay or plastic pot

BLOOM TIME
Various

Splash Petal Cattleyas
Orchid checklist:

✓ Grows on sunny windowsill
✓ Long-lasting flowers
✓ Sprays of multiple flowers
✓ Big flowers
✓ Great cut flower
✓ Noted for fragrance
✓ Attractive plant habit
✓ Once-a-week watering and fertilizer
✓ Repeat bloom
  Grows under fluorescent lights
✓ Grows easily into specimen

Some orchids become obsessions. I warn you: Splash Petal cattleyas may take over your life.

Splash Petals are clowns in the orchid world. The genetic phenomenon that causes color to "splash" from a flower's lip onto its petals is called *peloria*. What's happening is that the petals are trying to mimic the pollinator-attracting lip. Scientists term the aberrations "monstrous." In the *Cattleya* group, the effect is surprisingly beautiful, and hybridizers actively try to create more.

The palette range is an explosion of color, with two or three contrasting shades present simultaneously. The original splash petals were pink and white, but now include combinations of orange, red, purple, lavender, yellow, and green, from subtle to shocking.

Splashes come in a number of genera, labeled as *Brassolaeliocattleya*, *Cattleya*, *Guarisophleya*, *Laeliocattleya*, *Rhynchosophrocattleya*, *Sophrocattleya*, *Sophrolaeliocattleya*, and more. They're usually sold under the category of Splash Petal cattleyas.

I advise purchasing meristems (exact copies) of specific plants whose flowers appeal to you. Be dubious about the catalog words, *"hoping* for splash petals," in descriptions of hybrid crosses. Also be aware that even meristems sometimes aren't exact when too many are cloned.

Give them classic *Cattleya* culture: intermediate temperatures with a 10°F (5°C) drop at night in fall and winter, enough bright light so that leaves are a grassy light green, and a summer outdoors. Repot after bloom when the pot is outgrown.

Splash Petals usually flower once a year, but new hybrids often repeat bloom. Many are fragrant. Depending upon the cross, plant size can be compact to tall.

You'll covet them all.

Most Splash Petal orchids, including the ones pictured here, have their origin in *Cattleya intermedia* var. *aquinii*. Shown are *Guarisophleya* Mary Bui 'Peach Melba' (right), *Sophrocattleya* Purple Cascade 'Beauty of Perfume', HCC/AOS (inset, right), an unlabeled cultivar (inset, left), *Sophrocattleya* Mary Ellen Carter 'Dixie Hummingbird', HCC/AOS (page 25, bottom left), and *Thwaitesara* Perestroika (page 126).

Colmanara Wildcat

Wildcat Intergeneric Oncidium

PRONOUNCED
kole-man-AR-ah

ABBREVIATED
Colm.

CORRECTLY KNOWN AS
Odontocidium (Odcdm.) Wildcat

THE PLANT
Medium to large sympodial epiphyte; round flattish pseudobulb, wide grassy leaves, long spike of many patterned flowers

LIGHT NEEDS
Medium; eastern or southern window, under lights

TEMPERATURE RANGE
Intermediate; days 65–80°F (18–27°C), winter nights 55–62°F (13–17°C); tolerant

POTTING NEEDS
Medium orchid bark, plastic pot

BLOOM TIME
Two or three times a year, generally fall to winter

Colmanara Wildcat
Orchid checklist:

✓ Grows on sunny windowsill
✓ Long-lasting flowers
✓ Sprays of multiple flowers
✓ Big flowers
✓ Great cut flower
  Noted for fragrance
✓ Attractive plant habit
✓ Once-a-week watering and fertilizer
✓ Repeat bloom
✓ Grows under fluorescent lights
✓ Grows easily into specimen

Colmanara Wildcat is one of those orchids that seems to be everywhere. Give into temptation and buy it. It's easy, temperature-tolerant, and blooms freely in wild patterns and colors.

Wildcat can burst into arching and branching flower spikes, 2 ft. (0.6 m) long, each with forty to fifty big, butterfly-like blooms. Flowers are amazingly variable both in color and shape. The vividly contrasting shades are usually mahogany, red, yellow, and white, and adorned with bars, splotches, and/or picotees. The huge lips can be flamboyantly marked and ruffled. A display puts you in mind of jungle patterns, and many of the diverse cultivars are named for specific wild cats. Wildcat 'Bobcat', AM/AOS, for example, is one of the richest colored, more solidly dark, with deep red lip.

Wildcat often flowers twice yearly. Once mature enough, a plant can bloom for three months, rest for three, bloom for three, on a continual cycle.

Grow Wildcat in medium-bright light, avoiding hot direct sun, or under fluorescents. Keep the plant fairly moist, just drying slightly, and fertilize every week or two. It responds to good humidity; stand the plant on a pebble tray with water, but not sitting in water. Repot after bloom in late spring.

Colmanara Wildcat used to be considered a cross of *Miltonia* × *Odontoglossum* × *Oncidium*, but the *Miltonia* used was name-changed to an *Oncidium*. So now Wildcat is technically an *Odontocidium*. It's confusing. Wildcat's still widely available as *Colmanara*.

Wildcat is so popular I've even seen a video of it on YouTube. Join the fan club.

PARENTAGE: *Odontocidium* Wildcat (Rustic Bridge × Crowborough)

A very popular hybrid *Oncidium* intergeneric, *Colmanara* Wildcat (right) can bloom three or four times a year. 'Chadwick', AM/AOS (inset), is much less patterned than most varieties, which tend to have wild markings. 'Golden Red Star' is shown on page 9 (bottom).

Cymbidium Hybrids

Cymbidium

PRONOUNCED
sym-BID-ee-um

ABBREVIATED
Cym.

THE PLANT
Medium to large sympodial terrestrial; egglike pseudobulb, wide grassy leaves, tall sturdy spikes of waxy flowers

LIGHT NEEDS
High; southern window, sunroom, outdoors frost-free

TEMPERATURE RANGE
Cool to intermediate; days 60–80°F (16–27°C), winter nights 45–50°F (7–10°C)

POTTING NEEDS
Fine orchid mix, large deep plastic pot

BLOOM TIME
Winter to spring

Cymbidium Hybrids
Orchid checklist:

✓ Grows on sunny windowsill
✓ Long-lasting flowers
✓ Sprays of multiple flowers
✓ Big flowers
✓ Great cut flower
✓ Intensely colored or patterned
  Noted for fragrance
✓ Attractive plant habit
✓ Once-a-week watering and fertilizer
✓ Repeat bloom
  Grows under fluorescent lights
✓ Grows easily into specimen

The grassy-leaved *Cymbidium* is the oldest cultivated of all orchids. Confucius loved it. Just about any boxed corsage orchid is bound to be a *Cymbidium*. The incredible substance of the beautiful 3 in. (8 cm) wide bloom lasts for weeks when cut. The many-flowered spikes endure for months on the plant.

Cymbidiums are basically terrestrial orchids, meaning they grow in the ground instead of in trees. They prefer, therefore, to be in fine mix, in big pots, kept just moist. You can even grow them as landscape plants in the garden in frost-free areas.

These typically big plants are native from India to Japan to Australia, where they grow in high light and often very cool temperatures. High light and cool fall and winter nights are keys to getting them to bloom. Summer them outdoors until the first frosts. Then bring them to an unheated sunroom or a chilly sunny window. One friend sticks ice cubes on top of the mix in fall and winter to help cool the roots. Cymbidiums also respond to more fertilizer than many other orchids; use a solid slow-release such as Osmocote.

Because of the problem in finding a cool enough—and big enough—indoor spot for cymbidiums, there are shorter "miniature" hybrids, created using warmer-growing, fragrant types with starrier-shaped flowers, while others are cool-growers. Unfortunately, you usually can't tell if it's a miniature when you buy a small plant. Most are sold unlabeled. Be prepared for them to reach 3 ft. × 3 ft. (1 m × 1 m). If a plant stays a good windowsill size, it's a bonus.

The excellent *Cymbidium* color range includes white, pink, yellow, green, and brown, often with spotted and contrasting lips. Some examples are *Cymbidium* Ann Wilson (right), *Cymbidium* Alexalban (inset), and a mix of unlabeled hybrids (page 130). Miniature cymbidiums like the short Tiger Tail (page 9, second from top), a cool-growing *Cymbidium tigrinum* hybrid that blooms in spring, are a great choice for windowsills.

Degarmoara Flying High

Flying High Intergeneric Orchid

PRONOUNCED
de-gar-moe-AR-ah

ABBREVIATED
Dgmra.

CORRECTLY KNOWN AS
Bakerara (Bak.) Flying High

THE PLANT
Medium to large sympodial epiphyte; flat pseudobulb, wide grassy leaves, long arching sprays of yellow and brown starry blooms

LIGHT NEEDS
Medium; any window but northern

TEMPERATURE RANGE
Intermediate; days 60–85°F (16–29°C), winter nights 55–65°F (13–18°C); tolerant

POTTING NEEDS
Medium orchid mix, small plastic or clay pot

BLOOM TIME
Summer, can repeat

**Degarmoara Flying High
Orchid checklist:**

✓ Grows on sunny windowsill
✓ Long-lasting flowers
✓ Sprays of multiple flowers
✓ Big flowers
  Great cut flower
✓ Intensely colored or patterned
  Noted for fragrance
✓ Attractive plant habit
✓ Once-a-week watering and fertilizer
✓ Repeat bloom
  Grows under fluorescent lights
✓ Grows easily into specimen

I adore orchid species, but, as with cars, I also love good hybrids. Orchids that are created using lots of different types in their ancestry often result in easy-to-grow plants, tolerant of many conditions. The best have many eye-catching flowers that bloom repeatedly. Such a hybrid is Flying High.

Flying High belongs to the Oncidium group. Usually it's sold as *Degarmoara* Flying High, but because of taxonomic name changes, it's technically now *Bakerara* Flying High. In its background are the Spider Orchid (*Brassia*), Pansy Orchid (*Miltonia*), Dancing Lady (*Oncidium*), and Toothed Tongue Orchid (*Odontoglossum*). What you get is, well, a dancing pansy of a spider, with teeth.

The big, yellow and brown strongly marked flower dances with outstretched arms and legs, dressed in a huge skirtlike lip. There are often multiple spikes, with at least six well-spaced 4 in. (10 cm) long flowers on both sides of the arching spike, even on young plants.

To my eye, the best cultivar is the awarded 'Stars 'N Bars', AM/AOS, which has the deepest, most sophisticated color and patterning. The chrome yellow background of the petals and sepals is overlaid with mahogany red bars that look like they were drawn in a hurry with a fat marker. The creamy lip is dotted with big red spots and smaller speckles. Even the buds are pretty, deep yellow replete with stripes.

The attractive, grassy-leaved plant does well on any bright window, in average room temperatures, watered and fertilized weekly. Good humidity means more flowers.

The "toothed" aspect, by the way, is atop the lip, where two yellow canines sit as gap-toothed ornaments.

PARENTAGE: *Bakerara* Flying High (*Aliceara* Jet Setter × *Odontoglossum* McNabianum)

Degarmoara Flying High comes in cultivars that have much more yellow than 'Stars 'N Bars', AM/AOS (right), which is heavily marked with mahogany tones.

Dendrobium kingianum and Hybrids

Pink Rock Orchid, Captain King's Dendrobium

PRONOUNCED
den-DROH-bee-um king-ee-AN-um

ABBREVIATED
Den.

THE PLANT
Small to medium sympodial lithophyte; slender pseudobulb, leathery leaves, spray of small pink blooms

LIGHT NEEDS
Medium light; any window but northern

TEMPERATURE RANGE
Intermediate to cool; days 45–85°F (7–29°C), winter nights 50–65°F (10–18°C); very tolerant

POTTING NEEDS
Medium orchid mix, small plastic or clay pot

BLOOM TIME
Usually winter to spring; hybrids often repeat

Dendrobium kingianum and hybridsOrchid checklist:

✓ Grows on sunny windowsill
✓ Long-lasting flowers
✓ Sprays of multiple flowers
  Big flowers
  Great cut flower
✓ Noted for fragrance
✓ Attractive plant habit
  Once-a-week watering and fertilizer
✓ Repeat bloom
  Grows under fluorescent lights
✓ Grows easily into specimen

The compact and prolific Australian Pink Rock Orchid is one of the easiest orchids to grow. This species, which grows on rocks, is so variable in flower color and plant height that you might want to see one in bloom before you buy. But they're all adorable. And with 100 hybrids, there's a wealth of extended variety and flower form.

The classic 1 in. (2.5 cm) flower is pink, mauve, purple, or white, solid or in combination, as well as splash petal and picotee. The cute lip is often marked in contrasting color. There can be hundreds of flowers on an older plant, usually lightly scented of honey. Hybrids turn these winter-to-spring bloomers into anytime flowerers.

Dendrobium kingianum can quickly become a "passalong plant" because of its variable determination to create "keikis," or baby plants, that can be removed and potted up separately. You have some control over this. The plant wants a dry, unfertilized rest in autumn and winter. If you overwater it during these months, keikis appear instead of flowers. You can leave keikis on the plant, and it'll become a specimen bearing many flower spikes.

Grow it in a small pot in bright filtered light, at room temperature, keeping it just moist when it's actively growing, and fertilize weekly. Summer it outdoors. In fall, bring the plant inside, stop the water and fertilizer, and mist the leaves occasionally instead. It'll bloom best if the temperature then is 50°F (10°C).When you see buds, resume water; when it blooms, resume fertilizer.

Start with one. You'll never be out of gifts.

The honey-scented *Dendrobium kingianum* (right) from Australia can boast hundreds of pinkish flowers. It has a variety of color forms, and hybrids with other Australian orchids such as *Dendrobium speciosum* can even add yellow to the mix. *Dendrobium* Yondi (inset) is a yellow hybrid. The picotee variety is shown on page 6 (third from top).

Dendrobium nobile Hybrids

Noble, Softcane, or Yamamoto Dendrobium

PRONOUNCED
den-DROH-bee-um NOH-bih-lee

ABBREVIATED
Den.

THE PLANT
Medium to tall sympodial epiphyte; segmented cane stem, many vivid flowers on short stems along cane

LIGHT NEEDS
Medium to high; eastern or southern window, sunroom

TEMPERATURE RANGE
Warm summer days 70–85°F (21–29°C); two months of cold fall/winter nights 50–55°F (10–13°C)

POTTING NEEDS
Fine orchid bark, root-bound in tiny clay pots

BLOOM TIME
Generally January to May

Dendrobium nobile Hybrids
Orchid checklist:

Grows on sunny windowsill
✓ Long-lasting flowers
✓ Sprays of multiple flowers
✓ Big flowers
Great cut flower
✓ Intensely colored or patterned
✓ Noted for fragrance
✓ Attractive plant habit
Once-a-week watering and fertilizer
Repeat bloom
Grows under fluorescent lights
Grows easily into specimen

These are the spectacularly colored, contrast-throated, often unlabeled *Dendrobium* with nobbly bamboo-like canes, sold in bloom with many flowers arranged on short stems along the cane, that unwitting flower lovers take home and kill. It needn't be that way. Bred from *Dendrobium nobile*, these hybrids just need completely different care depending upon season, with a definite summer growing period after bloom, and a decided cool fall rest that's almost like hibernation.

The nicely scented flowers can last three months. Water weekly until bloom finishes, then step up watering to almost daily, using a low-nitrogen orchid fertilizer weekly throughout summer. Put the plant outside for summer in dappled light and leave it there until just before the first freeze in fall. *Dendrobium nobile* comes from Himalayan regions, and it can take it. The trick to bringing it inside is finding a cool spot so buds can form; a constant 55°F (13°C) has been proven to work well. If you don't have that, well, you're doomed, because tests show that if kept at 64°F (18°C) or above, Noble hybrids won't flower.

During this two- to three-month cool dry resting period, provide high light, but water only occasionally, with no fertilizer. Don't be dismayed to find the leaves dropping off, because it's normal. The cane nodules will then swell, and buds will eventually flower.

Orchid growers have a pet name for unlabeled *Dendrobium*, since it happens so often: NOID (no ID). If your unidentified *Dendrobium* flowers on long stems at the top instead of attached along the canes, you have a warmer-growing *Dendrobium phalaenopsis*.

Some of the most elegant and vivid orchids are *Dendrobium nobile* hybrids, but they need a cool dry rest in fall and winter. Shown here are *Dendrobium* Sailor Boy (right), and an unlabeled cultivar (left) affectionately called *Dendrobium* NOID for "no ID."

Dendrobium phalaenopsis Hybrids

Evergreen or Den-Phal Dendrobium

PRONOUNCED
den-DROH-bee-um fayl-eh-NOP-siss

ABBREVIATED
Den.

THE PLANT
Tall sympodial epiphyte; slender segmented stem with leafy tops, many white or purplish flowers on spikes at top

LIGHT NEEDS
High; any window but northern

TEMPERATURE RANGE
Warm; days 70–85°F (21–29°C), winter nights 65°F (18°C)

POTTING NEEDS
Medium orchid bark, root-bound in tiny clay pots

BLOOM TIME
Anytime; peak in fall

Dendrobium phalaenopsis
Hybrids Orchid checklist:

✓ Grows on sunny windowsill
✓ Long-lasting flowers
✓ Sprays of multiple flowers
✓ Big flowers
✓ Great cut flower
✓ Intensely colored or patterned
  Noted for fragrance
✓ Attractive plant habit
  Once-a-week watering and fertilizer
✓ Repeat bloom
  Grows under fluorescent lights
  Grows easily into specimen

One of the most common orchid plants at the supermarket is the *Dendrobium phalaenopsis* hybrid. The plants look rather like the "lucky bamboo" canes sold as houseplants, but with the addition of upright sprays of pretty, sometimes sweetly scented flowers at the very tops. The 2 to 3 in. (5 to 8 cm) blooms, which last several months, are usually white, lavender, or purple toned, although red, orange, yellow, chartreuse, and combinations are also available.

Dendrobium phalaenopsis are rather confusingly named, sharing "phalaenopsis" with another common yet unrelated orchid houseplant because the flowers are similar, but don't confuse the culture, because Den-Phals want more light, more water, and more fertilizer than *Phalaenopsis* Moth Orchids.

Unlike the *Dendrobium nobile* hybrids in the previous pages, with which they also can be confused, these Southeast Asian/Australian evergreens don't want a cool rest, although they do like to be a bit dry in winter. Grow them warm and in bright light year-round, keeping them moist during the summer, with weekly fertilizer. In the right amount of light, leaves are light green, not yellow and not dark, and sturdy instead of floppy.

In late summer or fall, you can help trigger flowering by reducing water slightly; the shortened day length will do the rest. Actually, you can try reducing day length almost anytime and the plant may respond with buds. They also respond to extra humidity; stand the pots on trays filled with pebbles and water.

Den-Phals have a Lazarus-like ability to bloom from even the most withered, leafless old cane, so don't rush to trim stems back.

Top-heavy Den-Phals bloom in tiny pots that tend to topple, so place them, pot and all, into a larger clay pot for ballast. Shown right is *Dendrobium* Polar Fire.

(inset) Dendrobiums are often unlabeled, as is the case with this all-white variety.

Disa Hybrids

Table Mountain Orchid, South African Orchid

PRONOUNCED
DEE-zah

ABBREVIATED
Disa

THE PLANT
Small sympodial terrestrial; underground tubers, short grassy leaves, tall flower spikes of multiple hooded blooms

LIGHT NEEDS
Medium; any window but northern, under lights

TEMPERATURE RANGE
Intermediate to cool; days 55–80°F (13–27°C), winter nights 45–60°F (7–16°C)

POTTING NEEDS
Sphagnum moss and perlite, or fine orchid mix, plastic pot

BLOOM TIME
Late spring to summer, can repeat in early winter

Disa Hybrids
Orchid checklist:

✓ Grows on sunny windowsill
✓ Long-lasting flowers
✓ Sprays of multiple flowers
✓ Big flowers
✓ Great cut flower
✓ Intensely colored or patterned
  Noted for fragrance
✓ Attractive plant habit
  Once-a-week watering and fertilizer
✓ Repeat bloom
✓ Grows under fluorescent lights
  Grows easily into specimen

From South Africa's Table Mountain comes a most dazzling orchid, named for the mythological Swedish goddess, Queen Disa. Spectacular new hybrids, as well as re-invigorations of older ones, are making these grassy streamside terrestrials popular.

Disa has an unusual, hooded, triangular flower shape, quite different than most other orchids. The colors, best in highest light, are fantastic neon red, orange, pink, peach, and yellow. They're grown commercially as cut flowers, lasting for weeks. Flower spikes can reach 2 ft. (0.6 m) high, and the 2 to 4 in. (5 to 10 cm) wide blooms last two months. Since they flower in June, imagine growing them for a wedding.

When it comes to *Disa* culture, you should almost forget these are orchids. I'd vote to change their common name to the *Un-Orchid* Orchid. They like water constantly, and can even sit in water, a no-no with virtually all other orchids. But—and this is key—they only like rainwater. And they hate being hot. If you can keep the roots cool in summer, and provide daily cool rainwater all year, definitely give *Disa* a try. Mine did fine under lights in a cool basement, with pots in trays where about 1 in. (2.5 cm) of water would collect, dilutely fertilized once a month. Other people report success in air-conditioned rooms.

Plants bloom while quite young. Repot after flowering, when you see new shoots, and water well. In winter, when new growth is going on underneath (they have tubers), you can stop fertilizing, and decrease water somewhat.

Scour the Internet if you must for the Goddess Un-Orchid.

Disa hybrids, such as the spotted Kewensis shown here (left), the peach forms of Unidiorosa (right), and the classic red of Riëtte (page 9, third from top), all have the red *Disa uniflora* in their ancestry, and provide a vibrant range of colors.

Encyclia cochleata

Cockleshell Orchid, Octopus Orchid

PRONOUNCED
en-SIK-lee-ah coke-lee-AH-tah

ABBREVIATED
Encycl. or *E.*

CORRECTLY KNOWN AS
Prosthechea (Psh.) cochleata

THE PLANT
Compact sympodial epiphyte; chubby oval pseudobulb, two leathery leaves, stem with multiple green-and-black blooms

LIGHT NEEDS
Low to medium; eastern window, under lights; adaptable

TEMPERATURE RANGE
Intermediate to warm; days 70–80°F (21–27°C), winter nights 58–65°F (14–18°C); adaptable

POTTING NEEDS
Medium orchid mix, clay pot

BLOOM TIME
Ever-blooming; peak in fall

Encyclia cochleata
Orchid checklist:

✓ **Grows on sunny windowsill**
✓ **Long-lasting flowers**
✓ **Sprays of multiple flowers**
  Big flowers
  Great cut flower
  Intensely colored or patterned
✓ **Noted for fragrance**
✓ **Attractive plant habit**
  Once-a-week watering and fertilizer
✓ **Repeat bloom**
✓ **Grows under fluorescent lights**
  Grows easily into specimen

Whenever people describe *Encyclia cochleata*, they invariably reach for words that have to do with the sea: cockleshell, clamshell, jellyfish, octopus—you get the idea. The 2.5 in. (6.4 cm) long flower is indeed shaped like an octopus, with a chocolate-black striped clamshell-like lip at the top for a head (which is the opposite orientation than most orchids), and light green petals and sepals that dangle down like twisted tentacles.

This is a very easy and adaptable orchid, beloved not only because of its intriguing shape, but also because it always seems to be in bloom. And I mean always; the flower spike can keep getting long, continually producing. I once saw one that was over 2 ft. (0.6 m) long on a mature plant with lots of growths. Don't be quick to cut it back when you think it's finished.

Most Cockleshell Orchids also have fragrant flowers, lightly scented of floral-lemons in the morning, kind of like air freshener.

Native from Florida (where it is endangered) to Central America, *Encyclia cochleata* is a slow grower, even though it flowers so continually. Grow this compact plant on an eastern window or under lights, water weekly or perhaps a bit more often, let it dry completely between water, and fertilize every two weeks. If it doesn't bloom, whether in natural or artificial light, move it somewhere where it gets more sun. I've also found it responds favorably to rainwater rather than tap.

This is almost an essential orchid, giving you at least one plant you can show off any time of the year.

Cockleshell Orchid, long known as *Encyclia cochleata*, has undergone a taxonomic name change to *Prosthechea cochleata* and may even be changed again, to *Anacheilium cochleatum*, demonstrating the volatility of botanical classification.

Iwanagara Appleblossom
Appleblossom Intergeneric Cattleya

PRONOUNCED
ee-wahn-ah-GAR-ah

ABBREVIATED
Iwan.

CORRECTLY KNOWN AS
Leonara (*Len.*) Appleblossom

THE PLANT
Medium sympodial epiphyte; long chubby pseudobulb, one to two leathery leaves, multiple fragrant *Cattleya*-like blooms

LIGHT NEEDS
Medium to high; any window but northern

TEMPERATURE RANGE
Intermediate; days 60–80°F (16–27°C), winter nights 55–60°F (13–16°C); very adaptable

POTTING NEEDS
Medium to coarse orchid mix, plastic or clay pot

BLOOM TIME
Anytime; often winter with summer repeat

Iwanagara Appleblossom Orchid checklist:

✓ Grows on sunny windowsill
✓ Long-lasting flowers
✓ Sprays of multiple flowers
✓ Big flowers
✓ Great cut flower
✓ Intensely colored or patterned
✓ Noted for fragrance
✓ Attractive plant habit
✓ Once-a-week watering and fertilizer
✓ Repeat bloom
  Grows under fluorescent lights
✓ Grows easily into specimen

This exquisite hybrid cross was man-made by combining, over time, an astonishing six different genera together: *Cattleya* × *Caularthron* × *Guarianthe* × *Laelia* × *Rhyncholaelia* × *Sophronitis*.

With all that in the background, instead of a great mess came the best of all worlds, a compact, repeat-blooming *Cattleya* type, usually in pastel two-toned picotee pinks with touches of yellow, although there are white, all-yellow, and all-pink types as well. The rather open, perky 3 in. (8 cm) wide flowers are wonderfully simple considering the genetic makeup, with sometimes six or more blooms beautifully presented above the leaves on each well-branched stem. Plants often bloom while still quite small, and flowering can go on for several months.

Then there's the fragrance, something worth bottling. I once saw it described as Lucky Charms cereal with orange peel added. The scent is most intense in morning, lingering into afternoon. I have heard complaints that sometimes there's no scent at all, which I guess is inevitable with such genetic diversity. But that's not the norm.

Appleblossom is adaptable and tolerant. Give it as much bright light as you can without burning the leaves, let it dry out between watering, fertilize weekly, and it should perform delightfully, rewarding you with charming flowers and fabulous fragrance. Repot after bloom when it outgrows the pot.

Sometimes this plant is found under the more accurate and newer name of *Leonara* Appleblossom, because botanists have rearranged many of its ancestral species into different categories, which has caused confusion in marketing. I've also seen it sold as Apple Blossom rather than the correct Appleblossom. Under whatever name you find it, grab it tightly and take it home.

PARENTAGE: *Leonara* Appleblossom (*Caulaelia* Snowflake × *Thwaitesara* Orange Nuggett)

The very fragrant Appleblossom hybrid cross is one that everyone seems to love, and it deservedly has won many awards.

Laeliocattleya Gold Digger

Gold Digger Intergeneric Cattleya

PRONOUNCED
lay-lee-oh-KAT-lee-ah

ABBREVIATED
Lc.

CORRECTLY KNOWN AS
Guarisophleya (Gsl.) Gold Digger

THE PLANT
Medium-sized sympodial epiphyte; long thickened pseudobulb, two leathery leaves, multiple *Cattleya*-like blooms

LIGHT NEEDS
Medium to high; eastern, southern, or western window

TEMPERATURE RANGE
Intermediate to warm; days 70–85°F (21–29°C), winter nights 60–65°F (16–18°C); adaptable

POTTING NEEDS
Medium to coarse orchid mix, plastic or clay pot

BLOOM TIME
Anytime, often in spring

Laeliocattleya Gold Digger Orchid checklist:

✓ Grows on sunny windowsill
✓ Long-lasting flowers
✓ Sprays of multiple flowers
✓ Big flowers
✓ Great cut flower
✓ Intensely colored or patterned
  Noted for fragrance
✓ Attractive plant habit
✓ Once-a-week watering and fertilizer
✓ Repeat bloom
  Grows under fluorescent lights
✓ Grows easily into specimen

Gold Digger is the epitome of cheerful. Even though this hybrid cross was created in 1974, it deservedly remains a very popular multi-floral *Cattleya*-type orchid. I think the most striking varieties are vividly colored yellow-gold with an obviously contrasting, solid red-hot lip, such as in the awarded cultivar 'Orchid Jungle', HCC/AOS. Others are more mandarin or yellow, with various degrees of red patterning in the lip. The more orange ones often open yellow, then gradually warm into a sunset tone.

Compact multi-florals such as Gold Digger are known for sprays of three or more flowers per spike, held upright over the plant as if they are flying. There are often quite a number of flower spikes, one per growth, a glorious sight when full of 3 in. (8 cm) wide blooms. Vigorous and adaptable, plants often flower while still small. The sprays make good cut flowers, but they'll last at least a month on the plant itself. Stick the pot into something really attractive and use the plant as a centerpiece.

Grow this hybrid in bright light on almost any window except a northern one, give it average home temperatures, but with a 10°F (5°C) drop at night during winter, water and fertilize weekly, and it's bound to be a reliable charmer, often with repeat bloom.

Gold Digger has undergone a name change, when some species in its parental background were taxonomically rearranged. Today, it is considered a mix of four genera: *Cattleya* × *Guarianthe* × *Laelia* × *Sophronitis*. Technically it's a *Gaurisophleya*, but mostly it's still sold as *Laeliocattleya*.

PARENTAGE: *Guarisophleya* Gold Digger (Red Gold × *Cattlianthe* Warpaint)

While some *Cattleya* types have big, fussy, frilly flowers, *Laeliocattleya* Gold Digger is charmingly simple and colorful. Shown here is 'Orchid Jungle', HCC/AOS.

Miltassia Charles M. Fitch

Charles M. Fitch Intergeneric Spider Orchid

PRONOUNCED
mil-TASS-ee-ah

ABBREVIATED
Mtssa.

THE PLANT
Medium sympodial epiphyte; long pseudobulb, grassy leaves, sprays of big lavender starry blooms

LIGHT NEEDS
Medium; eastern or southern window

TEMPERATURE RANGE
Intermediate; days 70–80°F (21–27°C), winter nights 55–60°F (13–16°C)

POTTING NEEDS
Fine orchid mix, plastic pot

BLOOM TIME
Fall to winter; can repeat

Miltassia Charles M. Fitch Orchid checklist:

✓ **Grows on sunny windowsill**
✓ **Long-lasting flowers**
✓ **Sprays of multiple flowers**
✓ **Big flowers**
  Great cut flower
✓ **Intensely colored or patterned**
  Noted for fragrance
✓ **Attractive plant habit**
  Once-a-week watering and fertilizer
✓ **Repeat bloom**
  Grows under fluorescent lights
  Grows easily into specimen

I love the easy-to-grow *Brassia* Spider Orchids with their long, arachnid-like parts, but they're mostly green and brown, and it'd be great to have more colorful ones. Obviously, someone else felt the same way. With the help of the hybridizer comes a mix between Spider Orchids and the more colorful Pansy Orchids (*Miltonia*). The result, *Miltassia*, is one of my favorite intergeneric types. I love the starry, big-lipped blooms.

I think the epitome is *Miltassia* Charles M. Fitch, an enduring cross from 1961. Its subtle, pale-green background is elegantly leopard-marked in rich lavender-purple, the large pansy lip toned in lilac. The markings are even evident on the outside of the long pointed buds. Over time, the pattern darkness on the flower fades to a pastel almost-gray, a wonderfully unexpected color, especially good combined with lilac-pink. I never met anyone who didn't think C. M. Fitch was drop-dead gorgeous.

The starry flowers stretch to 5 in. (13 cm), with a stellar presentation on long, multiple spikes. The blooms open sequentially and last two months.

I grow mine on a sunny eastern windowsill alongside *Cattleya* types, taking care that hot sun doesn't burn the thin, graceful, grassy leaves. It doesn't like extreme heat. Miltassias like humidity, and should be kept evenly moist so that the fine roots don't dry out; generally twice a week works well. Fertilize weekly when they are actively growing.

Charles M. Fitch is exceptionally vigorous, with a relatively compact plant habit. Flowers are huge compared to the plant size.

Miltassia crosses usually have huge, colorful lips, starry-shaped flowers, and long spidery petals and sepals, as seen here in *Miltassia* Charles M. Fitch 'Izumi', AM/AOS.

Miltonia

Pansy Orchid

PRONOUNCED
mil-TOH-nee-ah

ABBREVIATED
Milt.

THE PLANT
Compact sympodial epiphyte; flattish pseudobulb, grassy leaves, multiple pansy-like blooms

LIGHT NEEDS
Medium; eastern window, under lights

TEMPERATURE RANGE
Intermediate; days 65–80°F (18–27°C), winter nights 55–60°F (13–16°C)

POTTING NEEDS
Medium orchid mix, plastic pot

BLOOM TIME
One or two times a year, often summer

Miltonia
Orchid checklist:

✓ **Grows on sunny windowsill**
✓ **Long-lasting flowers**
✓ **Sprays of multiple flowers**
✓ **Big flowers**
  Great cut flower
  Noted for fragrance
✓ **Attractive plant habit**
✓ **Once-a-week watering and fertilizer**
✓ **Repeat bloom**
✓ **Grows under fluorescent lights**
  Grows easily into specimen

Pansy Orchids look like they belong in the garden, because they do resemble pansies, but pansies on steroids. Colors include pink, red, yellow, white, and purple, often in combination. The grassy-leaved plants are very pretty.

Pansy Orchids are actually a mix of two types that have been interbred extensively. The ones with very broad flowers and striking "waterfall" patterns on the lips are technically *Miltoniopsis*. Regardless, Pansy Orchids are almost always labeled just *Miltonia*.

If you have full, 3 in. (8 cm) long flowers with waterfall patterning, the plant has a lot of *Miltoniopsis* in it. If the bloom shape is more starry and less marked, it probably has more *Miltonia*. It's important to know this, because you grow the two types slightly differently. The *Miltoniopsis* waterfall-patterned one wants to be coddled more. Keep it 5°F (2–3°C) cooler than the recommended temperatures, in a bit lower light and in finer orchid mix, and water so it stays evenly moist instead of drying out somewhat in between. *Miltoniopsis* resents heat more than *Miltonia*, and grows under lights better. Fertilize both types twice a month.

All Pansy Orchids like to be repotted annually, immediately after blooming. Their fine roots are sensitive to sour conditions and too many salts, as well as too much or too little water. When things are going wrong with the roots, especially when too dry in either water or humidity, new leaves will "accordion" in pleats. Pay attention, and make remedies.

Miltonia makes terrible cut flowers, something I learned the hard way. Some of them are lightly scented of baby powder.

"Waterfall" lip patterns indicate that Pansy Orchids, like the unlabeled hybrid right and the pink hybrid on page 6 (top), need cooler conditions than types without such markings, such as *Miltonia* Bluntii (left).

Neostylis Lou Sneary

Lou Sneary Intergeneric Orchid

PRONOUNCED
nee-o-STY-liss

ABBREVIATED
Neost.

THE PLANT
Small monopodial epiphyte; arching alternate leaves, sprays of little blue-and-white flowers

LIGHT NEEDS
Medium; any window but northern, shielded from midday sun, under lights

TEMPERATURE RANGE
Intermediate; days 60–80°F (16–27°C), winter nights 55–60°F (13–16°C)

POTTING NEEDS
Medium to coarse orchid bark, clay pot

BLOOM TIME
Two or three times a year, often in summer

**Neostylis Lou Sneary
Orchid checklist:**

✓ Grows on sunny windowsill
✓ Long-lasting flowers
✓ Sprays of multiple flowers
  Big flowers
  Great cut flower
✓ Intensely colored or patterned
✓ Noted for fragrance
✓ Attractive plant habit
  Once-a-week watering and fertilizer
✓ Repeat bloom
✓ Grows under fluorescent lights
✓ Grows easily into specimen

Now here's a completely charming little plant, a hybrid between two equally charming *Vanda*-related parents, the Samurai Orchid (*Neofinetia falcata*) and a Foxtail Orchid (*Rhynchostylis coelestis*). Either one is also worth growing, especially for fragrance.

Lou Sneary's inheritance shows up well in its sprays of multiple 1 in. (2.5 cm) long, starry flowers with long nectar spurs, held brightly above pretty, arching leaves. The whole package makes a nice picture. My favorite color combination is the two-toned bluish lavender-and-white—the deep color is at the tips and in the vibrant lip. But they're all cute, whether two-toned pink-and-white, all pink, all white, all bluish. Blue is such a rare color in orchids, and in the horticultural world in general, that it's all the more appreciated when it actually happens—as it does with some Lou Snearys.

The blooms are fragrant, too, although, as sometimes is the case when both parents are extremely fragrant, the offspring can be a bit less strongly so. The fragrance does vary between plants. The scent, reminiscent of vanilla, sometimes citrusy, is lovely and notable, most pronounced in the evening.

A compact grower, Lou Sneary fits nicely on a bright windowsill protected from the strongest rays, and it's possible to bloom it under lights kept very close to the tubes. Water well when you see it actively growing, letting it dry slightly between. Fertilize weekly. In winter, let it dry a bit more.

Because of hybrid vigor, Lou Sneary can bloom two or three times a year, most reliably in warm months.

PARENTAGE: *Neostylis* Lou Sneary (*Neofinetia falcata* × *Rhynchostylis coelestis*)

The flowers of *Neostylis* Lou Sneary, whether two-toned, as shown on page 7 (second from top), or all one color, as in the pink cultivar 'Lea', AM/AOS, shown here, are adorable and fragrant.

Odontocidium Tiger Crow

Golden Girl Orchid, Tiger Crow Intergeneric Oncidium

PRONOUNCED
oh-don-toh-SID-ee-um

ABBREVIATED
Odcdm.

THE PLANT
Large sympodial epiphyte; long oval flattish pseudobulb, long wide grassy leaves, long sprays of spotted yellow flowers

LIGHT NEEDS
Medium; any window but northern, protected from afternoon sun

TEMPERATURE RANGE
Intermediate; days 65–80°F (18–27°C), winter nights 55–65°F (13–18°C); tolerant

POTTING NEEDS
Fine orchid mix, small clay or plastic pot

BLOOM TIME
Fall to winter, can repeat

Odontocidium Tiger Crow Orchid checklist:

✓ Grows on sunny windowsill
✓ Long-lasting flowers
✓ Sprays of multiple flowers
✓ Big flowers
✓ Great cut flower
✓ Intensely colored or patterned
✓ Noted for fragrance
✓ Attractive plant habit
  Once-a-week watering and fertilizer
✓ Repeat bloom
  Grows under fluorescent lights
✓ Grows easily into specimen

I've never seen a picture of Tiger Crow that did it justice. There's something about the clear buttery chrome yellow that eludes the camera, yet stops you in your tracks in person. The chocolate spots are sprightly, the fiddle-shaped lip big and bold. Even the dark pointed buds, with their tips tinted yellow, are arresting. This is a beautiful orchid.

The awarded 'Golden Girl', HCC/AOS, is the only cultivar generally available. I guess when you hit the jackpot, you stop spinning the wheel. Tiger Crow has two well-known *Odontocidium* parents, Tiger Hambühren and Crowborough. Both helped jump-start the craze for intergeneric *Oncidium* hybrids. The tolerant, easy-to-grow features are even better in Tiger Crow.

Lightly fragrant (kind of rosy), the 3 in. (8 cm) long flowers last for months.

The plant gets big fast, to 18 in. (46 cm) high, with 2 ft. (0.6 m) long branched flower spikes, each heavily laden with up to twenty-five blooms. Definitely stake them.

Tiger Crow isn't fussy about temperatures, but if nights drop to 55°F (13°C) for a few weeks, flower spikes often emerge. In fall, though, if you've summered it outdoors, emerging buds can dry up if suddenly subjected to the household heating system. Bring budding plants inside well before the heat is on.

Medium bright light, with only morning sun, suits it well. Leaves should be a bright green color. Water so the mix dries to 1 in. (2.5 cm) down (probably twice a week), and fertilize weekly. Once the growth is mature, reduce water and fertilizer a bit until you see new signs of life.

See Tiger Crow for yourself. You'll want one.

PARENTAGE: *Odontocidium* Tiger Crow (Tiger Hambühren × Crowborough)

A hybrid cross of two genera, *Oncidium* and *Odontoglossum*, *Odontocidium* in general is easy to grow, and *Odontocidium* Tiger Crow 'Golden Girl', HCC/AOS (right and page 3, middle), is a cheerful example.

Oncidium Gower Ramsey

Gower Ramsey Oncidium, Yellow Spray Orchid

PRONOUNCED
on-SID-ee-um

ABBREVIATED
Onc.

THE PLANT
Large sympodial epiphyte; flat oval pseudobulb, wide grassy leaves, very long multibranched sprays of little yellow flowers

LIGHT NEEDS
Medium; any window but northern, one hour of direct sun

TEMPERATURE RANGE
Intermediate; days 65–75°F (18–24°C), winter nights 55–60°F (13–16°C)

POTTING NEEDS
Medium orchid mix, small clay or plastic pot

BLOOM TIME
Fall, repeats in spring

Oncidium Gower Ramsey
Orchid checklist:

✓ Grows on sunny windowsill
✓ Long-lasting flowers
✓ Sprays of multiple flowers
  Big flowers
✓ Great cut flower
✓ Intensely colored or patterned
  Noted for fragrance
✓ Attractive plant habit
✓ Once-a-week watering and fertilizer
✓ Repeat bloom
  Grows under fluorescent lights
✓ Grows easily into specimen

Oncidiums are known for brilliant yellow blooms, and one of the most floriferous is the classic 1977 hybrid, Gower Ramsey. Robust and easy to grow, it has been mass produced, the decided standard for yellow spray *Oncidium*. Its 3 ft. (1 m) long multibranched spikes of little ballet dancers usually appear twice yearly, with a third show possible.

The blooms arrive in drifts, and the mass effect is fabulous. But check out the individual flowers, 1.5 in. (4 cm) high, spaced distinctly on erect spikes. Each resembles a woman wearing a vivid, big yellow skirt and donning a yellow hood striped in burgundy, her waist cinched in red, arms stretched to the sides, also striped in burgundy. She seems ready to pirouette. These dancers stick around for months.

Gower Ramsey's repeat bloom ability is legendary. Don't cut the spike if the tip is green, because more buds can develop and flower.

This hybrid was bred from the exceptionally vigorous Mexican/Central American Golden Shower Orchid, *Oncidium sphacelatum*. That's also worth growing if you have lots of room; its many growths can fill a bushel basket. Gower Ramsey is more manageable, although still big.

Grow Gower Ramsey in intermediate temperatures (if you err on temperature, go warmer rather than colder), and fertilize weekly, watering copiously but allowing it to dry in between. Avoid midday sun.

Look especially for the cultivar 'Volcano Queen', which has more substantial flowers on shorter, stronger spikes. An almost identical hybrid to Gower Ramsey is *Oncidium* Sweet Sugar (Aloha Iwanaga × *varicosum*), a shorter plant with slightly bigger, fuller flowers, also readily available.

PARENTAGE: *Oncidium* Gower Ramsey (Goldiana × Guinea Gold)

A famous yellow spray *Oncidium*, Gower Ramsey owes much to the Golden Shower Orchid (*Oncidium sphacelatum*), a species that predominates in its background.

(inset) Shorter but virtually identical to Gower Ramsey is *Oncidium* Sweet Sugar. Shown here is 'Million Dollar'.

Oncidium Sharry Baby

Chocolate Orchid, Sharry Baby Oncidium

PRONOUNCED
on-SID-ee-um

ABBREVIATED
Onc.

THE PLANT
Large sympodial epiphyte; flat egg-like pseudobulb, long wide grassy leaves, tall sprays of many small red-and-white fragrant flowers

LIGHT NEEDS
Medium; any window but northern, protected from afternoon sun

TEMPERATURE RANGE
Intermediate to warm; days 65–85°F (18–29°C), winter nights 60–65°F (16–18°C)

POTTING NEEDS
Fine orchid mix, small clay or plastic pot

BLOOM TIME
Peak in fall, can have spikes year-round

**Oncidium Sharry Baby
Orchid checklist:**

✓ Grows on sunny windowsill
✓ Long-lasting flowers
✓ Sprays of multiple flowers
  Big flowers
✓ Great cut flower
✓ Intensely colored or patterned
✓ Noted for fragrance
✓ Attractive plant habit
  Once-a-week watering and fertilizer
✓ Repeat bloom
  Grows under fluorescent lights
✓ Grows easily into specimen

Sharry Baby is one of the most popular orchid hybrids of all time, and the most popular *Oncidium*. Individually, the 1.5 in. (4 cm) red-and-white flowers aren't all that spectacular. Instead, Sharry Baby is famous for its powerful hot-chocolate-and-vanilla fragrance. This unbelievable scent, combined with a fantastic display from tall, flower-rich spikes, makes the easy-going Chocolate Orchid much beloved.

Like its diminutive cousin, *Oncidium* Twinkle, Sharry Baby shares the very fragrant ancestor, *Oncidium ornithorynchum*. Every Sharry Baby I've ever sniffed has been intensely fragrant. Scent is subjective; some insist there's no chocolate aroma, while generally agreeing on the vanilla. Flowers can be open a week before scent kicks in, strongest in the morning, especially when sitting in sun.

The awarded cultivar 'Sweet Fragrance', AM/AOS, is the best-known, while the more interesting 'Tricolor' adds yellow to the maroon-and-white palette.

Give Sharry Baby morning sun. It has a genetic trait of developing black spots on leaves when the light's too high; if the foliage is dark green, the light is too low. Water so the mix dries an inch (2.5 cm) down before re-watering, usually twice weekly. New growths shouldn't shrivel and leaves shouldn't "accordion"—if they do, increase watering, and mist it every morning. Fertilize weekly when actively growing, but reduce water and fertilizer in winter until you see new growth.

Drop the night temperature to 60°F (16°C) for several weeks to initiate the branched flower spikes. They can reach 3 ft. (1 m), so stake them upright as they grow.

Keep Sharry Baby under lock and key, or your friends will steal it.

PARENTAGE: *Oncidium* Sharry Baby (Jamie Sutton × Honolulu)

Strong chocolate aroma from a shower of many blooms will delight you for months. Shown here is the most popular variety, *Oncidium* Sharry Baby 'Sweet Fragrance', AM/AOS.

(inset) The addition of a third color to the standard *Oncidium* Sharry Baby is the highlight of the cultivar 'Tricolor'.

Oncidium Twinkle

Twinkle Oncidium

PRONOUNCED
on-SID-ee-um

ABBREVIATED
Onc.

THE PLANT
Small sympodial epiphyte; round-ish pseudobulb, short grassy leaves, branched sprays of tiny white, pink, or red flowers

LIGHT NEEDS
Medium; any window but north-ern, protected from hottest direct sun

TEMPERATURE RANGE
Intermediate; days 68–80°F (20–27°C), winter nights 55–65°F (13–18°C)

POTTING NEEDS
Fine orchid mix, small clay or plastic pot

BLOOM TIME
Fall, usually repeats in spring

Oncidium Twinkle
Orchid checklist:

✓ **Grows on sunny windowsill**
✓ **Long-lasting flowers**
✓ **Sprays of multiple flowers**
  Big flowers
  Great cut flower
✓ **Intensely colored or patterned**
✓ **Noted for fragrance**
✓ **Attractive plant habit**
  Once-a-week watering and fertilizer
✓ **Repeat bloom**
  Grows under fluorescent lights
✓ **Grows easily into specimen**

Cliches such as "cute as a button" actually don't seem so trite when you see *Oncidium* Twinkle in bloom. It's a lit-tle thing, under 10 in. (25 cm), with a profusion of flowers 0.5 in. (13 mm) or less in size. And then, just as you're admiring this compact effect, the evocative vanilla and spice fragrance hits your nose. Twinkle is irresistible.

This popular *Oncidium* pot plant is the product of two Cen-tral American parent species, and the perfume comes from *Oncidium ornithorhynchum*, a tolerant, lavender-flowered dar-ling which itself is worth growing. Twinkle comes in white, pink, red, or yellow, with yellow- or red-ridged lips. Scent is usually best in the white types, especially 'Fragrance Fantasy'. The white flowers are pink-flushed, and with age, the color whitens.

Warning: Twinkle will drive you crazy with its extremely long wait for the buds to open—they can take nearly six months from spiking until the cloud of little blooms appears. When Twinkle is grown well, it can easily make multiple flower spikes per growth, flower repeatedly, and double in size annually. The crowded growths bloom in a tiny pot.

Water Twinkle profusely and allow the mix to dry an inch (2.5 cm) down before watering again, but make sure it doesn't over-dry when in spike. Growths should be plump. If they wrinkle, you're not watering often enough. Twinkle also sulks if humidity is low, so use a humidity pebble tray underneath it. Fertilize every other week when it's growing, then reduce to monthly in winter. Repot each spring into a small pot.

Tiny, vanilla-scented fairy lights—that's Twinkle.

PARENTAGE: *Oncidium* Twinkle (*cheirophorum* × *ornitho-rhynchum*)

The profuse, tiny blooms of *Oncidium* Twinkle, like those of the cultivar 'Red Fantasy' seen here, are sweetly fragrant, and worth inspecting with a hand lens to see their complex form and intricate ridged lip.

(inset) The palest Twinkle varieties tend to be the most fragrant.

Oncidium varicosum

Dancing Lady Orchid

PRONOUNCED
on-SID-ee-um var-ee-KOE-sum

ABBREVIATED
Onc.

THE PLANT
Small sympodial epiphyte; ribbed pseudobulb, stiff leaf, spray of small yellow blooms

LIGHT NEEDS
Medium; any window but northern, under lights

TEMPERATURE RANGE
Intermediate to warm; days 65–90°F (18–32°C), winter nights 55–65°F (13–18°C)

POTTING NEEDS
Medium orchid bark, small clay or plastic pot

BLOOM TIME
Anytime, peak fall to early winter

**Oncidium varicosum
Orchid checklist:**

✓ **Grows on sunny windowsill**
✓ **Long-lasting flowers**
✓ **Sprays of multiple flowers**
  Big flowers
✓ **Great cut flower**
  Noted for fragrance
✓ **Attractive plant habit**
  Once-a-week watering and fertilizer
  Repeat bloom
✓ **Grows under fluorescent lights**
✓ **Grows easily into specimen**

*O*ncidium varicosum was the first *Oncidium* I ever grew. I was delighted not only by the many little, vibrant, yellow flowers that arrived reliably in fall, but also by the ease with which the compact plant grew. If you have a black thumb, try your inept hand at this one.

Many in the Oncidium group are dubbed "Dancing Ladies," but it fits this Brazilian species best. The branching flower spikes emerge from the bottom of the rough, spotted growth. Spikes reach 3 to 5 ft. (1 to 1.5 m) long, and from the middle onward can be a hundred 1 in. (2.5 cm) long sulfur yellow blooms. The little barred petals and sepals resemble the arms and head of a tiny senorita, atop the wavy-lipped skirt of a ballgown. The effect intensifies if you get the var. *rogersii*, because the ruffled lip dominating each flower is enormous.

Oncidium varicosum has been a great parent in more than 100 hybrid crosses, including Sweet Sugar, and it is a grandparent of Gower Ramsey. That huge lip is inherited, and often made bigger, but hybrid plant size is also larger. And it's the little plant habit of *Oncidium varicosum* that I cherish.

Dancing Lady grows well on a windowsill or under lights. If it doesn't bloom, it's probably not getting enough light, although it can balk if in excessive light. Let it go just barely dry between watering. Fertilize every other week when actively growing. When the new pseudobulbs are mature, reduce the water slightly and stop fertilizing until you see new growth.

So, go on, take a twirl with the original Dancing Lady.

The adorable yellow *Oncidium varicosum* var. *rogersii* has a bigger lip and more branches of flowers than the typical species. The plant is smaller and more manageable than many other yellow oncidiums.

Paphiopedilum, Complex Hybrids

Bulldog Paph, Bullfrog Ladyslipper

PRONOUNCED
paff-ee-oh-PED-ih-lum

ABBREVIATED
Paph.

THE PLANT
Compact sympodial terrestrial; rosette of green strap leaves, broad, big-pouched flower atop sturdy stem

LIGHT NEEDS
Medium; eastern window, under lights

TEMPERATURE RANGE
Intermediate; days 65–80°F (18–27°C), winter nights 55–60°F (13–16°C)

POTTING NEEDS
Fine orchid mix, small but deep plastic pot

BLOOM TIME
Generally winter

Paphiopedilum, Complex Hybrids Orchid checklist:

✓ Grows on sunny windowsill
✓ Long-lasting flowers
  Sprays of multiple flowers
✓ Big flowers
✓ Great cut flower
✓ Intensely colored or patterned
  Noted for fragrance
✓ Attractive plant habit
  Once-a-week watering and fertilizer
  Repeat bloom
✓ Grows under fluorescent lights
✓ Grows easily into specimen

Bulldog Paphiopedilums have been out of fashion after being all the rage from the 1800s to the 1960s. But these enormous, round, waxy flowers with the jowly look are back. The British, who love their English bulldogs, invented the complexly interbred hybrids that do remind you of those broad, sour mugs. One famous hybrid is even named for Winston Churchill; you can just imagine a cigar sticking out.

The huge, generally single flower, with classic ladyslipper-pouched lip, arises on a sturdy stem above solid green leaves. It absolutely does not look real. Bulldog Paphs mesmerize people: the comment I hear most is, "That *can't* be real." Even when touched, the flower is so substantial it feels like plastic.

Colors include yellow, green, brown, red, white, and pink, often with overlays, halos, spots, lines, and/or warts. Maybe it's the warts that earn them another nickname, Bullfrogs. Get one in bloom, even if it costs more, to ensure you like the look. If you buy a seedling from a hybrid cross, the colors and particularly the shape can be very variable. Some are downright homely, more like a toad than a bullfrog.

Easier to grow than their generations-ago ancestral species, these compact plants prefer cooler temperatures and more light than the Maudiae Paphs, similar to *Paphiopedilum primulinum*, both of which are also in this book. Complex Paph blooms are largest and most deeply colored when grown in their coolest temperatures. Give them small but deep pots that just hold the roots.

Your bulldog will mug in surreal perfection for at least a month, probably longer.

So waxy they seem plastic, Bulldog Paphs like *Paphiopedilum* Rosalie (right) and *Paphiopedilum* Farmingdale (inset) can be an acquired taste in tropical ladyslippers.

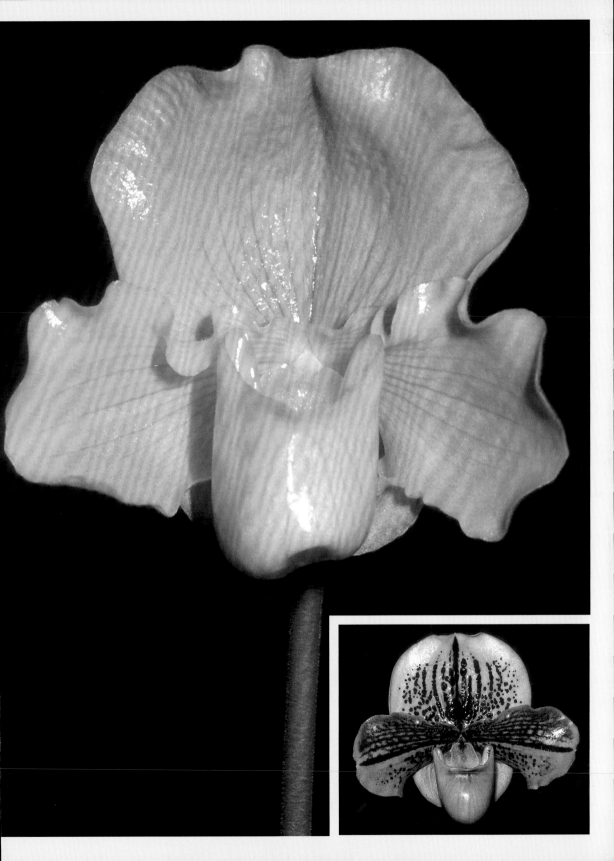

Paphiopedilum, Maudiae Hybrids

Maudiae Ladyslipper

PRONOUNCED
paff-ee-oh-PED-ih-lum MAW-dee-ay

ABBREVIATED
Paph.

THE PLANT
Compact sympodial terrestrial; rosette of pretty mottled leaves, big-pouched flower atop tall sturdy stem

LIGHT NEEDS
Low; eastern window, under lights

TEMPERATURE RANGE
Warm; days 70–85°F (21–29°C), winter nights 60–65°F (16–18°C)

POTTING NEEDS
Fine orchid mix, small but deep plastic pot

BLOOM TIME
Anytime; generally summer to fall

**Paphiopedilum Maudiae
Orchid checklist:**

✓ **Grows on sunny windowsill**
✓ **Long-lasting flowers**
   Sprays of multiple flowers
✓ **Big flowers**
   Great cut flower
✓ **Intensely colored or patterned**
   Noted for fragrance
✓ **Attractive plant habit**
   Once-a-week watering and fertilizer
   Repeat bloom
✓ **Grows under fluorescent lights**
✓ **Grows easily into specimen**

The Maudiae ladyslippers are among my favorite house-plant orchids. I constantly marvel at how such an exotic-looking flower, married to a really handsome marbled foliage, is so easy and dependable. I give them as gifts to people who don't grow orchids, especially if they disdain the ubiquitous *Phalaenopsis*. Your friends will fall into one of two *Paphiopedilum* camps: love 'em or hate 'em. Depends on the reaction to the lip pouch, I think.

Maudiae is actually just one of the hybrids in this general type, which trace origin to a terrestrial Asian species, *Paphiopedilum callosum*; they're sometimes called Callosum hybrids. All feature pretty mottled leaves—a honeycombed mix of light and dark green, or a more mottled dark and darker. The shiny, waxy, unreal-looking 3 to 5 in. (8 to 13 cm) long flower arises 10 in. (25 cm) above the plant. The bloom sports a big, striped upper sepal (the dorsal), two wart-and-bump covered petals that stick out like a handlebar mustache, and a deep big-pouched lip. Colors are usually green with white (the album form), with added pink (coloratum), or in such dark maroon they even approach black (vinicolor).

Grow these alongside *Phalaenopsis*, warm, allowing them to dry out just slightly between watering, and fertilize weekly. They do great under lights. Paphs like to be repotted yearly into fresh mix. Choose a pot that just accommodates the root mass.

There's usually a solitary flower per stem, although newer hybrids are producing up to five. The flower lasts months on end; one of mine once held out for nearly half a year.

PARENTAGE: *Paphiopedilum* Maudiae (*callosum × lawrenceanum*)

Paphiopedilum Maudiae ladyslippers generally are green with white, pink, or shades of maroon. Shown in both pictures is the album form. The coloratum variety can be seen on page 2. The beautiful mottled foliage of Maudiae-type paphiopedilums (left) is a bonus to the unique flower.

Paphiopedilum primulinum and Hybrids

Primrose Ladyslipper

PRONOUNCED
paff-ee-oh-PED-ih-lum prim-yoo-LYE-num

ABBREVIATED
Paph.

THE PLANT
Compact sympodial terrestrial; rosette of green strap leaves, yellow-pouched flower atop elongating stem

LIGHT NEEDS
Medium; any window but northern, under lights

TEMPERATURE RANGE
Intermediate to warm; days 60–85°F (16–29°C), winter nights 60–65°F (16–18°C)

POTTING NEEDS
Fine orchid mix, small but deep plastic pot

BLOOM TIME
Sequentially for a long time, often summer

Paphiopedilum primulinum and Hybrids Orchid checklist:

✓ Grows on sunny windowsill
✓ Long-lasting flowers
   Sprays of multiple flowers
✓ Big flowers
   Great cut flower
✓ Intensely colored or patterned
   Noted for fragrance
✓ Attractive plant habit
   Once-a-week watering and fertilizer
✓ Repeat bloom
✓ Grows under fluorescent lights
✓ Grows easily into specimen

Imagine a ladyslipper orchid that keeps blooming and blooming, one flower after another after another. Now quit imagining, because the easy-to-grow Primrose Ladyslipper is the real deal. I even know someone whose *Paphiopedilum primulinum* has been in nonstop flower for over two years.

This Sumatran species is named for its classic yellow primrose color, often coupled with green. There are darker, also very pretty forms with pink pouches. Except for a brief time when the next one is appearing, there's only one 2.5 in. (6.4 cm) long flower open at once. The flower isn't a grandstanding sort, but it's delicately cute, with ruffled sepals and shiny clear color. Its ability to keep blooming makes this a winning combination.

Paphiopedilums with solid green leaves such as this one, instead of mottled foliage like the Maudiae types, prefer more light and intermediate temperatures rather than warm. Sometimes called "strap-leaf" paphiopedilums, they can be grown alongside *Cattleya*. They are compact plants (except for the eventually long flower spike), and they even grow under lights. Water so that they stay just damp, about every four days, and fertilize weekly. Repot yearly after bloom, or when you start to see new leaves growing.

The *Paphiopedilum primulinum* flower spike eventually needs staking, because it keeps elongating, with a definite mind of its own. Each flower lasts several months.

Hybrids often create bigger flowers with fuller shapes, and sometimes more flowers open at once. Some to look for include the popular Pinocchio (pink and green), Golddollar (vibrant yellow), and the reliably two-flowered Becky Fouke (white or yellow).

Blooming sequentially for a very long time—sometimes years—the Primrose Ladyslipper and its hybrids are worth the little extra time to find a source. Shown here is *Paphiopedilum primulinum* forma *aureum* (with the next flower forming just before the previous one drops off) and its hybrid *Paphiopedilum* Pinocchio (inset). The hybrid Becky Fouke can be seen on page 8 (second from top).

Phalaenopsis, Big-Flowered Hybrids

Moth Orchid, Phal

PRONOUNCED
fayl-eh-NOP-siss

ABBREVIATED
Phal.

THE PLANT
Compact monopodial epiphyte; rosette of elongated oval leaves, long notched spike of multiple medium to large blooms

LIGHT NEEDS
Low; eastern window, under lights

TEMPERATURE RANGE
Warm; days 65–85°F (18–29°C), winter nights 60–65°F (16–18°C)

POTTING NEEDS
Medium orchid mix, plastic pot

BLOOM TIME
Anytime, peak winter to spring

Phalaenopsis,
Big-Flowered Hybrids
Orchid checklist:

✓ Grows on sunny windowsill
✓ Long-lasting flowers
✓ Sprays of multiple flowers
✓ Big flowers
✓ Great cut flower
✓ Intensely colored or patterned
  Noted for fragrance
✓ Attractive plant habit
✓ Once-a-week watering and fertilizer
✓ Repeat bloom
✓ Grows under fluorescent lights
✓ Grows easily into specimen

What?!! You don't own any *Phalaenopsis* orchids? The most popular potted plant in the United States after poinsettias? Go out right now and buy at least one. Here, take my car.

The Moth Orchid, so-dubbed because the flowers resemble flying moths, is the best beginner's orchid. The ubiquitous, large-flowered hybrids—often unlabeled—come in white, pink, red, purple, yellow, orange, solid, striped, or spotted. Each flower lasts easily a month. Plants can bloom half a year.

Phals are easy. Provide warm household temperatures that drop at night, and enough light so that the pretty leaves are grassy green, not dark. Repot annually into fresh mix after flowering, as your highest priority is to grow good roots.

The notched flower spike lengthens and forms buds that open successively in lovely presentation along two sides of the arching spike. That is, they present beautifully if you don't move the plant while buds develop. If its orientation to light changes, the flowers will skew in an irritating fashion. I mark the pot's bottom and its shelf with aligned pieces of tape. When the pot is moved for weekly watering at the sink, it's replaced in the same position. This works for any long-spiked orchid, by the way.

Don't cut the spike if the tip is still green; it'll keep producing. When flowering finally finishes, cut it above the second notch from the bottom, and it often reblooms. If yours doesn't, and it's getting enough light, drop the temperature 10°F (5°C) for two weeks.

Some *Phalaenopsis* are labeled *Doritaenopsis* (*Dtps.*). They're virtually the same thing.

Mostly native to the Philippines, the exceptionally easy Moth Orchid can be pristine white like this unlabeled variety (right), or come in an abundance of colors and patterns like *Phalaenopsis* Elegant Julia (inset), the yellow-toned Mystik Golden Leopard 'Cheetah', HCC/AOS (page 25, top right), or blushed like Maki Watanabe (page 8, top).

Phalaenopsis, Fragrant Novelties

Fragrant novelty Phalaenopsis

PRONOUNCED
fayl-eh-NOP-siss

ABBREVIATED
Phal.

THE PLANT
Compact monopodial epiphyte; rosette of elongated oval leaves, short to medium-length spikes of fragrant waxy blooms

LIGHT NEEDS
Low to medium; eastern window, under lights

TEMPERATURE RANGE
Warm; days 65–85°F (18–29°C), winter nights 60–65°F (16–18°C)

POTTING NEEDS
Medium orchid mix, plastic pot

BLOOM TIME
Various, usually winter

Phalaenopsis, Fragrant Novelties Orchid checklist:

✓ Grows on sunny windowsill
✓ Long-lasting flowers
  Sprays of multiple flowers
✓ Big flowers
✓ Great cut flower
✓ Intensely colored or patterned
✓ Noted for fragrance
✓ Attractive plant habit
✓ Once-a-week watering and fertilizer
  Repeat bloom
✓ Grows under fluorescent lights
  Grows easily into specimen

It comes as a great surprise to many people that some *Phalaenopsis* are fragrant. While there can be slight perfume to Moth Orchids—although usually not—others with a novel, waxy substance to their starrier blooms are delightfully scented.

Fragrant Phals stem from a few species. The two most famous are *Phalaenopsis violacea* and *Phalaenopsis bellina*, formerly considered color forms of *Phalaenopsis violacea* (*bellina* was previously the bicolored cream-and-violet Borneo variety, *violacea* the fuchsia Sumatran one). But *Phalaenopsis violacea* has a spicy cinnamon scent, while *Phalaenopsis bellina* smells like lily-of-the-valley.

Other fragrant species include *Phalaenopsis amboinensis*, a musky contender, and lilac-scented *Phalaenopsis lueddemanniana*. Both are vividly marked in yellow and red.

Hybridizers accidentally went into the perfume business by using these as parents. The goal, originally, was to brighten color, substance, and markings of large-flowered Moth Orchids, and improve flower count, shape, and short spikes of fragrant species. Sadly, however, as with many hybrid roses, the scent often disappeared. But in some glorious cases, perfume lingered. Generally, the closer a hybrid is to the original species, the more likely it is to be fragrant.

Grow them as you do other *Phalaenopsis*, although I give these a bit more light. Try not to leave water on the leaf crowns. The species tend to bloom their few flowers successively on the same spike, so don't be quick to cut it off.

Grow the species, of course. But also try hybrids Orchid World, Sweet Memory, and Brother Sara Gold, among others. Look for fragrant species on hybrid cross labels for likely prospects. Another good find is the recent line of breeding in *Phalaenopsis* Tzu Chiang Balm, which stays dwarf but with lots of fragrant flowers.

Perfumed Moth Orchids, like *Phalaenopsis* Brother Sara Gold (right), the Sumatran species *Phalaenopsis bellina* var. *alba* (inset), and *Phalaenopsis* Sweet Memory 'Bonnie Vasquez', AM/AOS (page 7, bottom), have long-lasting, vibrant blooms, often with fleshy substance and sunset tones.

Phalaenopsis, Multiflora Hybrids

Multiflora Moth Orchid, Sweetheart Phal

PRONOUNCED
fayl-eh-NOP-siss

ABBREVIATED
Phal.

THE PLANT
Compact monopodial epiphyte; rosette of oval leaves, branching spikes of multiple small-to-medium-sized blooms

LIGHT NEEDS
Low; eastern window, under lights

TEMPERATURE RANGE
Warm; days 65–85°F (18–29°C), winter nights 60–65°F (16–18°C)

POTTING NEEDS
Medium orchid mix, plastic pot

BLOOM TIME
Anytime, peak winter to spring

Phalaenopsis, Multiflora Hybrids Orchid checklist:

✓ Grows on sunny windowsill
✓ Long-lasting flowers
✓ Sprays of multiple flowers
  Big flowers
✓ Great cut flower
✓ Intensely colored or patterned
  Noted for fragrance
✓ Attractive plant habit
✓ Once-a-week watering and fertilizer
✓ Repeat bloom
✓ Grows under fluorescent lights
  Grows easily into specimen

How do you make a *Phalaenopsis* better? The question seems an oxymoron—isn't the Moth Orchid already wonderful? But what if there were more flowers (even if a bit smaller), on more stems, with plenty of branches, to give a real wow of a show? There are such cuties. They're called Multiflora Phals.

Compared with the Big-Flowered Moth Orchids, Multiflora *Phalaenopsis* (also known as Sweethearts Phals) are in relative infancy when it comes to hybridizing, only seriously since the 1980s. Most of them harken back to a branching little Philippine/Taiwan species, the darling *Phalaenopsis equestris*. Today, multifloras have evolved into bright colors, striped, blushed, and picoteed, with contrasting lips that often dominate the picture, and a flurry of flowers under 3 in. (8 cm) wide on smallish plants.

Because they are not ultra-hybridized obedient pets like their larger-flowered compatriots, multifloras tend to display their blooms in rather reckless orientations. I forgive them that. Actually, I like their wild hearts; it adds to the charm.

The green leaves on these compact plants often have purple undersides. They also fit better on windowsills and under lights. Grow them the same as the big Phals: warm temperatures, low light protected from burning sun, water and fertilize weekly. When the flower spike is brown at the tip, it is finished blooming, so cut it back above its second notch and it may reflower.

Some famous Multiflora Phal hybrids include Cassandra, Carmela's Pixie, Be Tris, Timothy Christopher, and their offspring. Even unlabeled, when in branched, smaller-flowered bloom, a multiflora will be clearly that. Grab it and run.

Multiflora Phals like *Phalaenopsis* Timothy Christopher (page 3, right) are sometimes just smaller, more branched and floriferous versions of classic white Moth Orchids, but usually they are more colorful, like Carmela's Pixie (right) and Be Tris (page 8, bottom).

Psychopsis papilio and Hybrids

Butterfly Orchid

PRONOUNCED
sye-KOP-siss pah-PILL-ee-oh

ABBREVIATED
Psychp. or *Pyp.*

ALSO KNOWN AS
Oncidium (Onc.) papilio

THE PLANT
Compact sympodial epiphyte; small, flat, dull-red pseudobulb, thick leaves spotted red, single big butterfly flower on very long stem

LIGHT NEEDS
Medium; any window but northern, protected from direct rays

TEMPERATURE RANGE
Warm; days 70–80°F (21–27°C), winter nights 58–60°F (14–16°C)

POTTING NEEDS
Medium to coarse orchid mix, small clay or plastic pot or basket

BLOOM TIME
Anytime; peak May to September

Psychopsis papilio and Hybrids Orchid checklist:

✓ **Grows on sunny windowsill**
✓ **Long-lasting flowers**
  Sprays of multiple flowers
✓ **Big flowers**
  Great cut flower
✓ **Intensely colored or patterned**
  Noted for fragrance
  Attractive plant habit
  Once-a-week watering and fertilizer
✓ **Repeat bloom**
  Grows under fluorescent lights
  Grows easily into specimen

You only get one of these amazing flowers at a time, but wow, is it worth it. Few orchid flowers make people screech to a halt like the flamboyant orange and yellow Butterfly Orchid.

With wavy-edged sepals that are evocative of a giraffe's patterning, the effect is made more arresting by the fact that the 6 in. (15 cm) long flower sits atop a ridiculously long stem, sometimes 5 ft. (1.5 m) above a 10 in. (25 cm) high plant. The bloom sits there for months, then produces others in succession after fading. This is one of those unique orchids that jump-started the Victorian passion for orchid growing in the 1800s.

I particularly like the antenna-like petals at the top of the flower, although I've never seen a butterfly with such long appendages. It's as if the bloom is dancing to the song, "Y.M.C.A."

Hybrids are similar, and can include gorgeous all-yellow (*alba*) types.

Native to the sides of trees in northern parts of South America, *Psychopsis papilio* prefers warm, cramped quarters in a small pot that's allowed to dry out between heavy summer watering, and weekly fertilizer. In winter, reduce water and fertilizer somewhat to let the plant rest. The Butterfly Orchid tends to resent repotting, and can grow undisturbed in the same pot for years if the mix doesn't break down too badly.

Since the long flower stem usually keeps growing and producing, don't cut it off when the flower fades, and you'll be treated to what sometimes seems like an eternity of sequential Butterfly Orchids waving in the breeze.

The summer-blooming phantasm known as the Butterfly Orchid, such as *Psychopsis papilio* (left) or the most highly awarded *Psychopsis* Mendenhall 'Hildos', FCC/AOS (right), can be in constant successive flower for years.

Rhynchostylis gigantea

Foxtail Orchid

PRONOUNCED
rink-oh-STY-liss ji-GAN-tee-ah

ABBREVIATED
Rhy.

THE PLANT
Tall monopodial epiphyte; coarse aerial roots, striped bright green alternating leaves, sturdy spike of many small pink-violet spotted flowers

LIGHT NEEDS
Medium; any window but northern, or sunroom, protected from direct sun

TEMPERATURE RANGE
Warm; days 70–95°F (21–35°C), winter nights 60–65°F (16–18°C); tolerant

POTTING NEEDS
Empty hanging slotted-wood basket, no mix

BLOOM TIME
December to March

**Rhynchostylis gigantea
Orchid checklist:**

✓ Grows on sunny windowsill
✓ Long-lasting flowers
✓ Sprays of multiple flowers
  Big flowers
  Great cut flower
✓ Intensely colored or patterned
✓ Noted for fragrance
✓ Attractive plant habit
✓ Once-a-week watering and fertilizer
  Repeat bloom
  Grows under fluorescent lights
✓ Grows easily into specimen

If they could speak, some orchids would have booming voices, and the Foxtail Orchid is definitely loud. This fabulous Thai/Indonesia-region species has as many as fifty densely-packed, waxy, vibrant, fuchsia-splashed pink flowers per stem, arising from 1 ft. (30 cm) long, thick, green-on-green striped leaves arranged in a fanlike plane. Below are lots of fat coarse roots that insist on sticking out all over. It's rather a pretty clown; you can almost visualize the rubber nose.

The capper—although you hardly need one—is the heady, richly spiced perfume, one that wins orchid-fragrance awards.

This is a great orchid for people who just can't keep their watering cans away from their plants, because it likes being anchored into a wooden basket without any mix, and then watered copiously every day. If you routinely kill orchids by overwatering, by all means, have a go at this one. Grow it warm year-round, in a bright spot shielded from direct sunlight, and fertilize weekly. What the Foxtail Orchid really responds to is high humidity and good air movement, and the more it has, the better both the growth and the flowering. It hates the air conditioning vent. Buy it a fan, and stick it outside for summer.

The flower spike is pendant (like a foxtail), another reason for using a hanging basket. *Rhynchostylis gigantea* resents repotting; leave it alone for years on end and it will grow into a multistemmed plant with hundreds of flowers.

There are pure red, white, and other color forms, but my favorite is the classic spotted jokester.

Striped leaves and a dense "foxtail" of vibrant, highly fragrant flowers are highlights of *Rhyncostylis gigantea* (right). Its scent is one of the best of all orchids, truly gorgeous.

Rossioglossum

Tiger Orchid, Clown Orchid

PRONOUNCED
ross-ee-oh-GLOSS-um

ABBREVIATED
Rssgls.

THE PLANT
Medium sympodial epiphyte;
round pseudobulb, two or three
broad leathery leaves, erect spray
of large striped flowers

LIGHT NEEDS
Medium to high; any window but
northern, protected from direct sun

TEMPERATURE RANGE
Intermediate to cool; days 60–80°F
(16–27°C), winter nights 50–60°F
(10–16°C)

POTTING NEEDS
Medium orchid mix, small clay or
plastic pot

BLOOM TIME
Fall to spring

Rossioglossum
Orchid checklist:

✓ **Grows on sunny windowsill**
✓ **Long-lasting flowers**
✓ **Sprays of multiple flowers**
✓ **Big flowers**
   Great cut flower
✓ **Intensely colored or patterned**
   Noted for fragrance
✓ **Attractive plant habit**
✓ **Once-a-week watering and fertilizer**
✓ **Repeat bloom**
   Grows under lights
   Grows easily into specimen

The obviously showy Tiger Orchid is so-dubbed because of red-brown striping on its vividly yellow sepals. It's also called the Clown Orchid, because if you look closely, right in the center of the flower there seems to be a helmet-hatted little clown. The huge, waxy, shiny blooms are fascinating no matter what your imagination conjures them to be.

Rossioglossum is a spectacular genus, with only six elite species, native from Mexico to Panama. The dramatic, long-lasting flowers can be enormous, especially in the best-known species, *Rossioglossum grande*, to 6 in. (15 cm) wide, four to eight on each spike.

Rossioglossum needs to grow very bright with no direct sun. If yours doesn't bloom, move the plant into more light. Water well but allow it to dry slightly in between, and fertilize weekly when in growth. *Rossioglossum* prefers to be warm during the day and cool at night, so give it a decided drop in nighttime temperature. Put it outdoors in late spring, until night temperatures drop below 50°F (10°C) in fall. In winter, after bloom, let it rest by reducing watering slightly, and stop fertilizing until summer.

The foot-long (30 cm) flower spike can get very heavy, so make sure to support it with a stout stake when it starts developing, clamped in several spots as it grows.

If you have a choice, buy the hybrid *Rossioglossum* Rawdon Jester (*grande* × *williamsianum*). It has wider petals and more vibrant flowers. Rawdon Jester is easier, more robust and temperature-tolerant, blooming twice yearly. It's sometimes incorrectly sold as *Odontoglossum* Rawdon Jester.

Tiger Orchid species *Rossioglossum schlieperianum* (right) is a more compact, temperature-tolerant version of the popular *Rossioglossum grande* (left). At the center of each flower, a little clown-like figure can be seen.

Sarcochilus

Ravine Orchid

PRONOUNCED
sar-koe-KYE-lus

ABBREVIATED
Sarco.

THE PLANT
Compact monopodial lithophyte; slender alternating leaves, sprays of little flowers

LIGHT NEEDS
Medium; eastern or southern window

TEMPERATURE RANGE
Intermediate to cool; days 55–85°F (13–29°C), winter nights 40–55°F (4–13°C)

POTTING NEEDS
Coarse orchid mix or rocks, shallow clay or plastic pot

BLOOM TIME
Spring to summer

Sarcochilus
Orchid checklist:

✓ **Grows on sunny windowsill**
✓ **Long-lasting flowers**
✓ **Sprays of multiple flowers**
   Big flowers
   Great cut flower
✓ **Intensely colored or patterned**
✓ **Noted for fragrance**
✓ **Attractive plant habit**
   Once-a-week watering and fertilizer
   Repeat bloom
   Grows under fluorescent lights
✓ **Grows easily into specimen**

Australia is home to some absolutely adorable orchids. The crystalline little blooms on compact, pretty, easy-to-grow plants make the Ravine Orchid one of the cutest.

Related to Vandas but infinitely smaller, most of the species used in hybridizing grow atop rocks. Lightly fragrant, *Sarcochilus* blooms easily. Multiple flower spikes are typical, each with up to 25 flowers. Flowers vary greatly even within a species, but are mostly white with red and gold, or pink to red.

You're more likely to find hybrids rather than species. *Sarcochilus* Fitzhart (*hartmannii* × *fitzgeraldii*) is the most famous. It produces many 1.5 in. (4 cm) wide white flowers with red and yellow at the centers. Fitzhart is a robust plant that grows faster than either parent, with larger flowers. It blooms when very young.

Newer hybrids offer gorgeous color combinations such as burgundy on white, and include white, pink, dark red, or green, with spots or bars, often brightly colored yellow and red in the lip. The spikes can cascade like dense little tails, dangling 6 to 10 in. (15 to 25 cm) long.

Ravine Orchids grow where it gets cold in winter, and even take some frost. Temperature-tolerant, they're fine in warm summers, but need to drop to at least 55°F (13°C) on winter nights. Keep them just moist, and water in the morning in winter so they will dry faster and avoid fungal disease. Fertilize weekly when actively growing. Higher humidity will mean better growth and more flowers, and good air movement will prevent most problems. Give red hybrids a bit more light.

Warning: if snails or slugs appear, they'll head straight for *Sarcochilus*. Pick them off at night.

Probably the most robust of the Ravine Orchids is the hybrid *Sarcochilus* Fitzhart (right). Its flowers can vary widely between plants, as can be seen in another Fitzhart cultivar (page 7, third from top).

Schomburgkia and Hybrids

Schomburgkia, Schombocatts, Schombo Hybrids

PRONOUNCED
shom-BERG-kee-ah

ABBREVIATED
Schom.

THE PLANT
Large sympodial epiphyte; hollow, bamboo-like pseudobulb, two or three thick leaves, long flower spikes of twisted, neon flowers

LIGHT NEEDS
High; southern window, can take full sun

TEMPERATURE RANGE
Intermediate to warm; days 65–85°F (18–29°C), winter nights 55–65°F (13–18°C)

POTTING NEEDS
Medium orchid bark, clay pot or wooden basket

BLOOM TIME
Variable

Schomburgkia and Hybrids
Orchid checklist:

✓ Grows on sunny windowsill
✓ Long-lasting flowers
✓ Sprays of multiple flowers
✓ Big flowers
✓ Great cut flower
　 Noted for fragrance
　 Attractive plant habit
✓ Once-a-week watering and fertilizer
　 Repeat bloom
　 Grows under fluorescent lights
✓ Grows easily into specimen

Here's a *Cattleya*-related genus that's becoming trendy, especially since some hybridizers are ramping up its use to create a new line of often wildly twisted, strongly colored *Cattleya* types. You're going to see a lot more of them.

The convoluted and curled *Schomburgkia* flowers often look like someone stuck them in an electric light socket. If Kramer from *Seinfeld* were an orchid, he'd be *Schomburgkia undulata*—big, gangly, and frizzled. Depending upon what's crossed with what, the hybrids can be nothing short of fantastic.

The flower spike on *Schomburgkia* can reach an amazing 6 ft. (1.8 m) long. It's only at the end that you'll find the clusters of 3 to 4 in. (8 to 10 cm) wide, shiny, vibrant, sometimes fragrant flowers.

Schomburgkia is native to the tropical Americas, where its hollow stemlike pseudobulbs are home to specialized ants, which in turn provide the plant with fertilizer. Some species get enormous—a single pseudobulb can be 4 in. (10 cm) wide. They need a huge amount of light, and are perfect outdoors in places like Florida.

The extremely diverse hybrid plants are smaller—often much smaller—more manageable, and less demanding. If you're in less sun-drenched parts of the world, save yourself some angst and buy hybrids. Look for names such as *Schombolaelia*, *Schombocattleya*, *Maclemoreara*, *Myrmecocattleya*, and *Recchara*. They may likely just be called Schombocatts or Schombo hybrids.

Grow Schombo hybrids in higher light than usual for *Cattleya* types. While yellowed leaves usually indicate that an orchid is getting too much light, this is not so with *Schomburgkia*. They're normally yellow when grown well.

Ah, the cutting edge. Try a Schombo hybrid.

The Schombocatt hybrid *Recchara* Frances Fox (right) mixes *Brassavola*, *Cattleya*, *Laelia*, and *Schomburgkia*.

(inset) *Schomburgkia undulata* has the waviest of flowers, a riveting sight that seems lit up by neon.

Sedirea japonica

Japanese Sedirea, Nago-ran

PRONOUNCED
seh-DEHR-ee-ah juh-PAWN-ih-kah

ABBREVIATED
Sdr. or *Sed.*

THE PLANT
Miniature monopodial epiphyte; rosette of alternating leaves, small cream blooms

LIGHT NEEDS
Medium; eastern or southern window, under lights

TEMPERATURE RANGE
Intermediate; days 65–80°F (18–27°C), winter nights 50–55°F (10–13°C

POTTING NEEDS
Fine orchid mix or sphagnum moss, small clay or plastic pot

BLOOM TIME
Winter to spring, sometimes summer

Sedirea japonica
Orchid checklist:

✓ **Grows on sunny windowsill**
✓ **Long-lasting flowers**
✓ **Sprays of multiple flowers**
  Big flowers
  Great cut flower
  Intensely colored or patterned
✓ **Noted for fragrance**
✓ **Attractive plant habit**
✓ **Once-a-week watering and fertilizer**
✓ **Repeat bloom**
✓ **Grows under fluorescent lights**
  Grows easily into specimen

I love miniature orchid plants, and the Japanese Sedirea fits not only that category, but also the incredibly fragrant list. Sweet and lemony, the scent persists at all hours. The diminutive 6 in. (15 cm) high plant, with its sprays of pretty little blooms, makes a tidy little picture. It deserves a beautiful little pot.

The creamy or greenish flowers usually have magenta lip markings as well as barring on the bottom sepals. It's not unusual to see two 6 in. (15 cm) long flower spikes at once, bearing up to a dozen waxy blooms. The 1 in. (2.5 cm) high flowers hold themselves cupped forward, and provide a nice two-month show.

The plant resembles a tiny *Phalaenopsis*, but don't make the mistake of growing it like one. Nago-ran, which is what it's called in its native southern Japan ("ran" means orchid), needs to be grown cooler and in more light than Phals. *Cattleya*-type bright light works well. Give it a six-month fall to winter cooling period, with night temperatures around 50°F (10°C). Place the plant right against the window in winter, especially if you've got one where the insulation quality isn't that great.

When it's in active growth, water Nago-ran as the mix is just beginning to dry out, every few days, and fertilize every other week. If it fusses, try rainwater. In winter, reduce the watering slightly, but don't let it dry out too much. Repot every year in spring.

Sedirea japonica can sit for quite a while, especially in winter, seemingly dormant, without any signs of new growth. Give it time.

Sedirea is actually *Aerides* spelled backwards, a taxonomic joke. *Aerides* was the genus in which this orchid was originally classified, before scientists changed their minds. The fragrant flowers of *Sedirea japonica* sparkle with crystalline light.

Sophrolaeliocattleya Jewel Box

Jewel Box Cattleya

PRONOUNCED
soff-roe-lay-lee-oh-KAT-lee-ah

ABBREVIATED
Slc.

CORRECTLY KNOWN AS
Guarisophleya (*Gsl.*) Jewel Box

THE PLANT
Compact sympodial epiphyte; slender pseudobulb, two leathery leaves, sprays of brilliant red flowers

LIGHT NEEDS
Medium; eastern or southern window

TEMPERATURE RANGE
Intermediate; days 65–85°F (18–29°C), winter nights 55–65°F (13–18°C); tolerant

POTTING NEEDS
Medium orchid mix, plastic or clay pot

BLOOM TIME
Winter to spring, often Valentine's Day

Sophrolaeliocattleya Jewel Box Orchid checklist:

✓ Grows on sunny windowsill
✓ Long-lasting flowers
✓ Sprays of multiple flowers
✓ Big flowers
✓ Great cut flower
✓ Intensely colored or patterned
  Noted for fragrance
✓ Attractive plant habit
  Once-a-week watering and fertilizer
✓ Repeat bloom
  Grows under fluorescent lights
✓ Grows easily into specimen

*C*attleya orchids can be tall and gawky, so it was to great acclaim when hybridizers starting creating "compact Catts" that had lots of decent-sized flowers yet stayed more modest in plant height. Jewel Box dates to the early 1960s, making it an oldie, but a goodie. They're still making truckloads of them, not only because it's compact and the dark red color is fantastic, but also because it often conveniently and appropriately blooms around Valentine's Day. It's a vigorous treasure.

Jewel Box owes a lot to the wonderful influence of its parent *Cattleya aurantiaca*, which lends many clusters of vibrantly colored blooms, each held a little forward. But Jewel Box has much bigger flowers, about 4 in. (10 cm) long, three or four in a cluster. The red sepals are long and pointed, while the lip and the petals, also red, are ruffled.

Give the plant medium light, a bit brighter than other *Cattleya*—it flowers best with direct morning sun, protected from hot afternoon rays. Provide more water than that given a typical *Cattleya*, perhaps every five days, and fertilize every other watering. Jewel Box does fine even if cooler or warmer than recommended, but it flowers better if it gets a 10°F (5°C) drop in temperature for a few weeks in fall. It can bloom twice yearly.

There are a number of cultivars, usually red, some orange. They're all good.

Sophrolaeliocattleya Jewel Box is now technically *Guarisophleya* Jewel Box because of taxonomic renamings. But after all these years of great performance, it's hard to call it anything else.

PARENTAGE: *Guarisophleya* Jewel Box (*Guarianthe aurantiaca* × *Sophrocattleya* Anzac)

Sprays of lots of vivid red flowers on compact plants make Jewel Box an essential, easy, reliable orchid, and excellent for corsages. Shown here is *Sophrolaeliocattleya* Jewel Box 'Dark Waters', AM/AOS.

Tolumnia Hybrids
Equitant Oncidium

PRONOUNCED
toe-LUM-nee-ah

ABBREVIATED
Tolu.

ALSO KNOWN AS
Oncidium (Onc.)

THE PLANT
Tiny sympodial epiphyte; fanlike array of triangular leaves, long spray of colorful little blooms

LIGHT NEEDS
Medium to high; southern or western window

TEMPERATURE RANGE
Warm; days 70–90°F (21–32°C), winter nights 60–70°F (16–21°C)

POTTING NEEDS
Medium to large orchid bark with charcoal pieces, or no mix, tiny clay pot

BLOOM TIME
Anytime, peak autumn or spring, often repeat

Tolumnia Hybrids
Orchid checklist:

✓ Grows on sunny windowsill
✓ Long-lasting flowers
✓ Sprays of multiple flowers
  Big flowers
✓ Great cut flower
✓ Intensely colored or patterned
  Noted for fragrance
✓ Attractive plant habit
  Once-a-week watering and fertilizer
✓ Repeat bloom
  Grows under fluorescent lights
  Grows easily into specimen

The flowers of Equitant *Oncidium* are small, but they pack a huge wallop of vivid color. Their brightly toned lips are like skirts at a salsa dance, a riot of movement. It's fitting, because *Tolumnia* hails from the Caribbean.

With fans of three-sided leaves, Tolumnias are miniature orchids less than 6 in. (15 cm) high. Yet the flower spike can be 1 ft. (30 cm) long, bearing many quarter inch (19 mm) long blooms at the end. Don't cut it when flowering finishes. It can branch and keep on producing.

Healthy roots are truly key to growing Equitants. The potting mix must never become mushy, and needs to drain quickly, drying out completely between watering. You can even grow these orchids in clay pots with no mix. Water potted plants every other morning when actively growing; water daily those with no mix. Fertilize only lightly, once a month. Reduce both a bit in winter. Watch closely for attacks by scale, treating outbreaks quickly with insecticidal soap.

If yours doesn't bloom, there's probably not enough light; the leaves should be tinted red at the edges. Also keep it warm, but drop the temperatures 5°F (2–3°C) at night.

Some people find Equitants hard to grow, and invariably it's because the humidity is too low. Keep plants away from drying radiators and air conditioners, stand the pots on pebble trays of water, and add daily misting. A fan is also useful. They don't do well if divided, and resent repotting.

Equitants can refuse to grow for a while when first brought home. Indulge them. They'll reward you with jewels.

Bright yellow, red, pink, and orange tones highlight the diminutive Equitants, which are usually sold under their correct name, *Tolumnia*, rather than as *Oncidium*. Shown here are a mix of Genting hybrids (right) and Golden Sunset (left). Genting Sunshine is on page 24.

Vanda Hybrids

Vanda

PRONOUNCED
VAN-dah

ABBREVIATED
V.

THE PLANT
Tall monopodial epiphyte; many coarse aerial roots, strap or pencil-like opposite leaves, big neon-colored flowers on sturdy stem

LIGHT NEEDS
High; southern window

TEMPERATURE RANGE
Warm; days 70–90°F (21–32°C), winter nights 60–75°F (16–24°C)

POTTING NEEDS
Coarse orchid bark or none, wooden baskets

BLOOM TIME
Anytime; up to three times a year

Vanda Hybrids
Orchid checklist:

✓ **Grows on sunny windowsill**
✓ **Long-lasting flowers**
✓ **Sprays of multiple flowers**
✓ **Big flowers**
  Great cut flower
✓ **Noted for fragrance**
  Attractive plant habit
  Once-a-week watering and fertilizer
✓ **Repeat bloom**
  Grows under fluorescent lights
✓ **Grows easily into specimen**

Humid South Pacific tropics are home to many *Vanda* species. Predictably, these exceptionally colorful plants do best in high sunlight and warm humid temperatures. Growing them in Florida or Hawaii is a snap. In less sunny areas, they're not as happy, but hybrids help make the transition; an especially good intergeneric hybrid option is *Ascocenda*.

Available in a dizzying array of sparkling colors, Vandas themselves even include that rare horticultural shade of blue. Blue or yellow hybrids often are more temperature-tolerant, since they stem from cooler environs. But, generally, the warmer the environment, the faster Vandas grow.

The 2 to 4 in. (8 to 10 cm) long extremely showy flowers have a mesmerizing crystalline shine. Flowers are sometimes fragrant and generally last three weeks. The thick flower spike has multiple blooms, and often emerges near the fifth leaf from the top, with multiple blooms.

Provide the sunniest indoor spot, and a summer outdoors, making a gradual transition to full sun to avoid sunburn. Water daily, and fertilize weekly. Indoor misting helps.

The vinelike, gawky plant usually looks beat-up. Its tangle of stiff roots is almost an entity by itself, sticking out in the air and hanging down in long strands to the ground. Because of this, grow *Vanda* in a slatted wooden basket, filled with coarse orchid bark or even empty. In spring, you can dislodge and repot the easily broken roots by soaking them for hours first. Better still, just put the old basket into a bigger one and avoid damage.

Vandas typically need to be fairly big to flower, but when they do, you'll want a grass skirt.

Brilliant pink, orange, red, green, white, purple, and even true blue can be found in *Vanda* flowers. Shown here is *Vanda* Manuvadee 'Sky', FCC/AOS, and *Vanda* Motes Buttercup (inset). *Vanda* Rubymoon can be seen on page 3.

Vuylstekeara Cambria

Cambria Intergeneric Orchid

PRONOUNCED
vuyl-steek-uh-AR-ah

ABBREVIATED
Vuyl.

THE PLANT
Medium sympodial epiphyte; flat oval pseudobulb, grassy leaves, arching spike of vibrant red-and-white butterfly-like blooms

LIGHT NEEDS
Low to medium; any window with early morning sun except northern, under lights

TEMPERATURE RANGE
Intermediate to cool; days 60–80°F (16–27°C), winter nights 50–60°F (10–16°C)

POTTING NEEDS
Medium orchid mix, small plastic or clay pot

BLOOM TIME
Fall to winter, often repeats

Vuylstekeara Cambria
Orchid checklist:

✓ **Grows on sunny windowsill**
✓ **Long-lasting flowers**
✓ **Sprays of multiple flowers**
✓ **Big flowers**
　Great cut flower
✓ **Intensely colored or patterned**
　Noted for fragrance
✓ **Attractive plant habit**
　Once-a-week watering and fertilizer
✓ **Repeat bloom**
✓ **Grows under fluorescent lights**
✓ **Grows easily into specimen**

It's got a tongue-twisting name I know we mispronounce. Have a native Belgian speak it for you. Bet you still won't be able to say it correctly. It's named for the first man to combine three *Oncidium*-related genera. Charles Vuylsteke created *Vuylstekeara* in 1912, which includes one of the most famous, mass-produced orchid hybrids.

Cambria is so well-known that people often mistakenly call all *Vuylstekeara* the Cambria Orchid. First bloomed in 1931, Cambria is still widely sold.

The cultivar 'Plush', FCC/AOS, is considered the finest, a highest-awarded, vibrant red-and-white sparkler. The elegant form is just about perfect, with wide, symmetrical, richly red parts coupled with an extraordinary pansy-like white lip artistically painted and spotted in red. There's a bright yellow, ridged crest right in the center.

You can sometimes find other Cambrias, usually with a strongly contrasted mix of red and white on the petals and sepals. There is even a gorgeous, albeit tough-to-find, orange Cambria.

The genus *Vuylstekeara* is a mix of *Cochlioda*, *Miltonia*, and *Odontoglossum*, which generally are cooler-growing. Cambria itself tends to be temperature-tolerant, but err on the side of cool rather than warm. Grow it in filtered light, so leaves don't sunburn, or under lights. Keep it well-watered during active growth, just barely drying out, and fertilize every other week. In winter, reduce water and fertilizer slightly. Cambria responds to increased humidity, and a fan helps keep fungal problems at bay.

The beautifully presented, arching sprays of 3.5 in. (9 cm) long flowers are so eye-catching that Cambria is an irresistible impulse purchase.

PARENTAGE: *Vuylstekeara* Cambria (Rudra × *Odontoglossum* Clonius)

Vuylstekeara Cambria (right) is one of the most popular hybrid orchids in the world and you may even find somewhat similar types mistakenly labeled Cambria. *Vuylstekeara* Cambria 'Plush', FCC/AOS (page 6, second from top), is considered one of the finest of this hybrid cross.

Wilsonara Red Pacific

Red Pacific Intergeneric Orchid

PRONOUNCED
wil-son-AR-ah

ABBREVIATED
Wils.

THE PLANT
Medium sympodial epiphyte; oval pseudobulb, four grassy leaves, long branched spray of deep red flowers

LIGHT NEEDS
Medium light; eastern window

TEMPERATURE RANGE
Intermediate; days 65–80°F (18–27°C), winter nights 55–60°F (13–16°C), very tolerant

POTTING NEEDS
Medium orchid mix, small plastic pot

BLOOM TIME
Fall, repeats in spring

Wilsonara Red Pacific
Orchid checklist:

✓ **Grows on sunny windowsill**
✓ **Long-lasting flowers**
✓ **Sprays of multiple flowers**
✓ **Big flowers**
  Great cut flower
✓ **Intensely colored or patterned**
  Noted for fragrance
✓ **Attractive plant habit**
✓ **Once-a-week watering and fertilizer**
✓ **Repeat bloom**
  Grows under fluorescent lights
✓ **Grows easily into specimen**

You'd think hybridizers might tire of the various ways they can combine different types within the *Oncidium* group of orchids. But no—here's yet another man-made intergeneric. *Wilsonara* blends the red Snail Orchid (*Cochlioda*) with the vivid patterns of the Toothed Tongue Orchid (*Odontoglossum*), and flings in yellow Dancing Lady (*Oncidium*) to boot. You get tolerant hybrid vigor, which is rather the point of it all.

There are plenty of nice crosses, but one I discovered recently was bred from the famous *Colmanara* Wildcat, using the almost solid red cultivar, 'Bobcat', AM/AOS. The all-red *Wilsonara* Red Pacific is shaping up to make its mother proud.

The cultivar to get is the awarded 'Deep Shadows', HCC/AOS. The 2 in. (5 cm) long, roundish flower is an extraordinary color for an *Oncidium* type: velvety blood-red in the petals and sepals, a bright red ruffled lip with raised teeth at the top, and punctuated with an eye-catching white anther cap right in the center. The blooms last about six weeks and make a pretty picture with the bright green 1 in. (2.5 cm) wide grassy foliage that, unfortunately, my cat likes to munch.

Red Pacific races to be an adult, incredibly fast to grow, and flowers while very young. A first bloom can have twenty-five flowers on each 1.5 ft. (4 m) long branched spike, and usually throws multiple spikes.

Grow *Wilsonara* in a small pot, grouped with other orchids atop a humidity pebble tray. Water copiously about once a week, perhaps more, so that it just about dries out. Fertilize weekly. Red Pacific tolerates more warmth than many other intergenerics of its type.

PARENTAGE: *Wilsonara* Red Pacific (*Odontocidium* Wildcat × Lisa Devos)

Wilsonara is another in the group of intergeneric orchids, like *Aliceara, Beallara, Burrageara, Colmanara, Degarmoara,* and *Vuylstekeara,* that blend at least three different *Oncidium* types together. Shown here and on page 10 is *Wilsonara* Red Pacific 'Deep Shadows', HCC/AOS.

Zygopetalum and Hybrids

Zygopetalum

Zygopetalum
Orchid checklist:

✓ Grows on sunny windowsill
✓ Long-lasting flowers
✓ Sprays of multiple flowers
✓ Big flowers
✓ Great cut flower
✓ Intensely colored or patterned
✓ Noted for fragrance
✓ Attractive plant habit
  Once-a-week watering and fertilizer
  Repeat bloom
  Grows under fluorescent lights
✓ Grows easily into specimen

I don't know why *Zygopetalum* isn't on everyone's windowsill. It's one of my favorite orchids. I'm on a crusade to have everyone appreciate it.

Okay, not everyone adores the shiny purple, brown, and green coloration, although vibrant fuchsia lips and wonderful patterning should compensate. But fragrance is what catapults *Zygopetalum* into the stratosphere.

This is one of the great perfumes of the orchid world. You will smell it several rooms away—an intense mix of baby powder and hyacinths. I once observed an orchid fragrance judging with professional perfumers, where the scent of *Zygopetalum* was described as "indole, linalool, and benzaldehyde," which sounds disheartening, yet clearly the perfumers were wild about it. So am I.

The long-lasting multiple 3 in. (8 cm) blooms, beautifully spaced along sturdy stems, are grown commercially in the cut flower trade.

Also get the new intergeneric hybrid *Zygolum* Louisendorf (*Zygosepalum labiosum* × *Zygopetalum* Artur Elle), still fabulously fragrant, but on a smaller plant.

Grow all types in bright light protected from hot temperatures, hanging from a tree in summer. If growth is spindly, there's not enough light; leaves should be light green. Water so plants never quite go dry, and lightly fertilize monthly; reduce both in winter. If leaf tips turn black, there's either too much fertilizer or salts from tap water. Reduce fertilizing and flush the pots monthly with distilled or rain water. Roots are soft and fragile, so repot carefully, using shallow pots.

Zygopetalum is my canary in the coal mine: if the air is stale and stagnant, its pretty, thin leaves spot, and whitefly appears. Pay attention—it means the air's not that good for you either. Treat yourselves both to a humidifier and a fan.

Zygopetalum Blackii (right), the newer intergeneric hybrid *Zygolum* Louisendorf (inset), and *Zygopetalum* Helen-Ku (page 7, top), like all the very day fragrant South American zygopetalums, whether hybrid or species, are easy to grow.

DECODING ORCHID NAME ABBREVIATIONS

Often, what you'll find on an orchid label is an incomprehensible abbreviation, or a mix of incomprehensible abbreviations. This chart will help you decode what kind of orchid you have, and whether it is a naturally occurring genus, or an intergeneric hybrid one. If it's a hybrid genus, listed also are the genera that are used in creating it.

All of the following have been mentioned in this book. Included are genus names that are technically outdated, but still commonly found on labels.

ABBREVIATION	GENUS	NATURAL OR HYBRID
Ada	*Ada*	Natural
Alcra.	*Aliceara*	Brs. × Milt. × Onc.
Angcm.	*Angraecum*	Natural
Ascda.	*Ascocenda*	Asctm. × V.
Asctm.	*Ascocentrum*	Natural
B.	*Brassavola*	Natural
Bak.	*Bakerara*	Brs. × Milt. × Odm. × Onc.
Bapt.	*Baptistonia*	Natural
Blc.	*Brassolaeliocattleya*	B. × La. × C.
Bllra.	*Beallara*	Brs. × Cda. × Milt. × Odm.
Bnts.	*Brassosophronitis*	B. × Soph.
Brs.	*Brassia*	Natural
Brsa.	*Brassada*	Ada × Brs.
Brsdm.	*Brassidium*	Brs. × Onc.
Burr.	*Burrageara*	Cda. × Milt. × Odm. × Onc.
C.	*Cattleya*	Natural
Cda.	*Cochlioda*	Natural
Cll.	*Caulaelia*	Clrthr. × L.

ABBREVIATION	GENUS	NATURAL OR HYBRID
Clrthr. or *Cau.*	*Caularthron*	Natural
Colm.	*Colmanara*	*Milt.* × *Odm.* × *Onc.*
Ctt.	*Cattlianthe*	*C.* × *G.*
Cym.	*Cymbidium*	Natural
Den.	*Dendrobium*	Natural
Dgrma.	*Degarmoara*	*Brs.* × *Milt.* × *Odm.*
Diacm.	*Diacrium*	Natural (now *Clrthr.*)
Dial.	*Dialaelia*	*Diacm.* × *L.* (*Cll.*)
Disa	*Disa*	Natural
Dor.	*Doritis*	Natural
Dtps.	*Doritaenopsis*	*Dor.* × *Phal.*
Encycl. or *E.*	*Encyclia*	Natural
G. or *Gur.*	*Guarianthe*	Natural
Gsl.	*Guarisophleya*	*C.* × *G.* × *Soph.*
Iwan.	*Iwanagara*	*B.* × *C.* × *Diacm.* × *L.*
L.	*Laelia*	Natural
Lc.	*Laeliocattleya*	*C.* × *L.*
Len.	*Leonara*	*C.* × *Clrthr.* × *G.* × *L.* × *Rhynch.* × *Soph.*
Mclmra.	*Maclemoreara*	*B.* × *L.* × *Schom.*
Mcp.	*Myrmecophilia*	Natural
Milt.	*Miltonia*	Natural
Mltnps. or *Mps.*	*Miltoniopsis*	Natural
Mtssa.	*Miltassia*	*Brs.* × *Milt.*
Myc.	*Myrmecocattleya*	*C.* × *Mcp.*
Neof.	*Neofinetia*	Natural
Neost.	*Neostylis*	*Neof.* × *Rhy.*
Odbrs.	*Odontobrassia*	*Brs.* × *Odm.*
Odcdm.	*Odontocidium*	*Odm.* × *Onc.*

ABBREVIATION	GENUS	NATURAL OR HYBRID
Odm.	*Odontoglossum*	Natural
Onc.	*Oncidium*	Natural
Paph.	*Paphiopedilum*	Natural
Phal.	*Phalaenopsis*	Natural
Psh.	*Prosthechea*	Natural
Psychp. or *Pyp.*	*Psychopsis*	Natural
Recc.	*Recchara*	*B.* × *C.* × *L.* × *Schom.*
Rhy.	*Rhynchostylis*	Natural
Rhynch. or *Rl.*	*Rhyncholaelia*	Natural
Rolf.	*Rolfeara*	*B.* × *C.* × *Soph.*
Rsc.	*Rhynchosophrocattleya*	*C.* × *Rhynch.* × *Soph.*
Rssgls.	*Rossioglossum*	Natural
Sarco.	*Sarcochilus*	Natural
Sc.	*Sophrocattleya*	*C.* × *Soph.*
Schom.	*Schomburgkia*	Natural
Sdr. or *Sed.*	*Sedirea*	Natural
Slc.	*Sophrolaeliocattleya*	*C.* × *L.* × *Soph.*
Smbc.	*Schombocattleya*	*C.* × *Schom.*
Smbl.	*Schombolaelia*	*L.* × *Schom.*
Soph. or *S.*	*Sophronitis*	Natural
Thw.	*Thwaitesara*	*C.* × *G.* × *L.* × *Rhynch.* × *Soph.*
Tolu.	*Tolumnia*	Natural
V.	*Vanda*	Natural
Vuyl.	*Vuylstekeara*	*Cda.* × *Milt.* × *Odm.*
Wils.	Wilsonara	*Cda.* × *Odm.* × *Onc.*
Z.	Zygopetalum	Natural
Zglm.	*Zygolum*	*Z.* × *Zspm.*
Zspm.	*Zygosepalum*	Natural

FOR MORE INFORMATION

I heartily recommend you join the international American Orchid Society, or give a membership as a gift. Everyone from beginners to expert growers will appreciate the monthly, all-color *Orchids* magazine, and access to the members-only section of the AOS Web site and its vibrant Orchid Forum, where you can read and post messages. You also get many discounts on books and supplies and admissions to over 200 botanical gardens. The AOS will put you in touch with your local member society—there are hundreds, all over the world—which has enjoyable monthly meetings with orchid displays, lectures, plant trades and sales, and in-person help with your questions. It's a great way to make friends while fueling your orchid passion. Because, as I often say, orchids are like potato chips. Betcha can't have just one.

American Orchid Society
16700 AOS Lane
Delray Beach, FL 33446-4351
Telephone: 561-404-2000
Email: TheAOS@aos.org
Web site: www.aos.org

Cymbidium

ABOUT THE AUTHOR

Photograph by Graham Rice.

judywhite is author and photographer of the award-winning *Taylor's Guide to Orchids* (Houghton Mifflin 1996). A past trustee of the American Orchid Society (AOS), she has earned its highest prize for writing about orchid culture, as well as the AOS Silver Medal for outstanding service to the orchid community.

Her photography has graced many books and publications, and has been exhibited at the Smithsonian Institution.

A former research biologist and past editor-in-chief of one of the world's first mega-gardening Web sites, Time Life's Virtual Garden, judywhite is married to British garden writer Graham Rice. The pair divides their time between rural Pennsylvania and Northamptonshire, England. She is proud to say she has killed orchids on both sides of the Atlantic.

Visit her Web site at www.gardenphotos.com.